Insane Success!

Mom & Dad,
You've supported and encouraged me in all my pursuits. What do you know one actually happened. ♡ u

Steph Londino

Psalm 71:14

Praise For Insane Success!

Written in these pages is a vulnerable look at the journey we are called to walk, this necessary falling up into a pain-filled yet grace-filled place, where healing can begin, and true freedom is found. As Mr. Lomelino shares, what we initially may perceive as suffocating failure can guide us, if we choose to open to it, to a place of examining our idols. What do we truly value, and why? This, in turn, can lead us more deeply to humility, grace, and freedom through surrender. Through sharing his own story, along with numerous spiritual and practical applications, Mr. Lomelino shows that trusting God fully allows us to experience the courage to let go of falseness and pride, and the courage to listen and to allow ourselves to say 'yes!' to who we are truly made to be. This, he purports, is the 'insane' success to be found in living a life that appears counter to the upward climb valued by much of our society. This book will be an indispensable guide for those struggling on the journey, and also for those that walk alongside in love, teaching the value of community, connection, and acceptance.

—Kim Pollock

Insane Success!

From Losing the American Dream to Finding God's Abundant Life

By Steven Lomelino
Edited by Jeanette Windle

ISBN 978-1-5465249-7-7

Visit Author at www.liveafterloss.blogspot.com

Cover Design by Rob Williams at fiverr.com/cal5086
Author Photo by Elizabeth Holliker, Flash Focus Imagery LLC at www.flashfocusimagery.com

Scripture taken from:
NEW LIVING TRANSLATION (NLT): Scripture quotations are taken from the Holy Bible, New Living Translation, copyright ©1996, 2004, 2007, 2013, 2015 by Tyndale House Foundation. Used by permission of Tyndale House Publishers, Inc., Carol Stream, Illinois 60188. All rights reserved.

ENGLISH STANDARD VERSION (ESV): Scripture quotations are from the ESV® Bible (The Holy Bible, English Standard Version®), copyright © 2001 by Crossway, a publishing ministry of Good News Publishers. Used by permission. All rights reserved.

KING JAMES VERSION: English translation of the Christian Bible for the Church of England begun in 1604 and completed in 1611.

1 3 5 7 9 10 8 6 4 2
Printed in the United States of America

Dedication

To my wife, Brenda, without whom I would have allowed loss, injustice, and fear keep me from finding a life worth writing about.

Thank you for allowing me to share our darkest days to help others find the way through theirs.

Love you, Ladybug.

Acknowledgements

Les "Sarge" Morgan – *you supported my pursuit of the impossible from day one; occasionally motivating me with the promise of a butt kicking if I gave up. Sorry, Brenda is still the better motivator. Details inside.*

Doris "Dodie" Morgan – *You got stuck reading my raw first attempt at making sense of a time I couldn't think straight. Thanks for encouraging me to keep writing.*

Scott Owens – *Thanks for the "Don't tell God no" advice.*

Lydia Beaman – *Encourager, prayer warrior.*

Kentucky Christian Writers Conference Staff – *You made me feel welcome, comfortable, and quickly put my fears that I didn't belong to rest.*

Jeanette Windle – *Long distance tutor extraordinaire.*

Amy Deardon – *Thanks for all the behind the scenes detail work to produce the final product and make it available to the world.*

***Jesus** – Thank You for redeeming my past by choosing the most inept person to share your message of hope. You brought the people listed above, and all mentioned within these pages, alongside me at just the right moment. All the glory to You, Lord, for all that is accomplished through these words.*

Table of Contents

Insane Success!

INTRODUCTION
NO, NO, AND NO!

November 4, 2004. A day I don't want to remember and one I will never forget. That was the day I made plans to drive out of my hometown of Springfield in central Illinois and never return. Though at the time I truly believed I'd stopped living for myself and begun living for Christ, that day proved I had not. On November 4, 2004, I gave the same one-word answer to my employer, to my wife, and to God.

"Steven Lomelino, make a presentation on our new computer communication tool."

No!

"Steven Lomelino, do you want to talk to Brenda?"

No!

"Steven Lomelino, you've acknowledged me as your Savior. You now see that so much of life is out of your control.

Do you trust Me to take control? Will you surrender your life fully into My care today? Will you also acknowledge me as your Lord?"

No, no, and—as much as I know I should—no!

I was not yet ready to admit that my own drive for status and material possessions had led me to this place. That my attempts to recreate what God had allowed to get swept away had been absolutely futile. That my plans for attaining a life of abundance and earthly success had not just failed miserably, but were so completely shattered, I saw no possibility of mending them. Even less was I ready to admit that God's definition of success might just be different from my own.

But hitting absolute bottom on that dreadful day of despair, November 4, 2004, as insane thoughts turned to senseless action, proved not to be the ending of my life journey. It proved instead to be a beginning. The beginning of a journey to understanding the insanity of a life dedicated only to attaining material success. There are those who may call insane a life focused on giving over having. On living joyfully despite depressing circumstances. I've discovered that such a life is truly the greatest form of success.

If you've ever hit rock-bottom, wondered where God is in the midst of failure, doubted God's presence, or if God even cares enough to have a divine plan for your life, then join me on my own journey to redefining real success. Along the way, you'll discover as I have a radically different, freeing life, its ultimate outcome far better than our human effort can attain. That's success God's way. That's amazing success. That's ***Insane Success***!

CHAPTER ONE
ALL IS GONE!

I know what it's like to be dead—at least as much as anyone can who is still living. By late fall/winter of 2004, the mind-numbing injustice of my employment life had become too much for me to take. I could not get a mental grasp on the fact that a job into which I'd invested a good part of my adult working life no longer existed. The leadership of two companies had come to an agreement that turned my own life upside-down. Was I supposed to just move on like it was no big deal? Like it was nothing personal?

I'm sure the objective of those company leaders wasn't to destroy their employees' lives. In fact, many of the other employees may have landed firmly on their feet. Not me. I'd landed flat on my back. Over and over, the same angry thoughts churned through my mind. I'd worked my way up from the bottom for that job. I'd fought through panic attacks that had put me in the hospital to keep that job. I'd agreed to meet with psychiatrists to keep that job. I'd found my self-confidence and a job I'd looked forward to staying in for the long haul. I'd earned equal status with higher-ranked coworkers.

To sum it up, I'd found my perfect stair on the employment staircase. Then just two weeks later, it had crumbled away beneath my feet. My wonderful "long-haul" new position had been eliminated. My job was history. It was all gone, just gone! Call it what you want, but when you make an employee start over after having already paid his dues to make something of himself, it sure feels personal.

That was 1998. By 2004, one might think plenty of time had passed to put one lost job behind me. But I had no desire to work anywhere except the hard-earned niche I'd carved out for myself, and that place no longer existed. Even if not intentional, that setback still felt a major injustice, a wound that time had not healed.

To make matters worse, my own improper responses to that job loss had led only to one failure after another, causing the initial sense of injury to grow deeper with each passing day. It's no wonder I felt that my efforts no longer mattered. Nothing would compare to what had been pulled out from under me. Success was eluding me despite all my efforts to recapture it.

Four years after finding and losing my perfect plateau, my desire to climb *any* employment stairs was gone. Though I'd found a job to which I was expected to show up each day, I had less and less desire to do anything. I'd been accustomed to walking into work with my head held high and walking out with it held even higher. Now I walked in half-confident and walked out each day even less confident.

A main reason for this was the huge gap between employer expectations and the minimal training and resources I'd been provided with to meet those expectations. Why would an employer set me up to fail? That hardly made sense, yet I was clearly not being granted the training or resources to succeed. I'd previously ascended multiple flights of employment stairs so naturally and easily. Why wasn't that same approach working now?

I have no idea how I kept going in that mental condition for so long, but it was another full two years before matters came to a head. The only thing I can come up with regarding those last two years is that I was hoping for someone or something to stop my slow downward spiral. But nothing did. I eventually reached the point where my emotions were completely spent. I felt only an unfillable void with nothing left of me but a physical shell. Even worse, I felt abandoned by God, my spirit utterly disillusioned.

By this time, I had lost all expectation of ever regaining any type of employment that would come close in prestige or financial remuneration to what I'd had before. Though I continued going through the motions, I found it harder and harder to maintain the charade of convincing people around me that I had any hope of things improving. My hope was gone—just gone!

Eventually something had to give. Of all places, I gave way to despair at a church prayer meeting on November 3rd, 2004. To everyone else in attendance, it was a normal late-autumn evening in Southern View, a township of Springfield. I had become very good at covering up my feelings, but how was it no one noticed that I was emotionless? That despite a thin veil of normalness I'd been able to place over my despair,

I was unable to truly enjoy anything? Didn't they see the same empty eyes screaming *I'm dead* that I saw every time I dared look closely at myself in the mirror?

Deep down, I wanted someone to notice I wasn't just feeling down, but was feeling nothing. I was inwardly dead. If only I could tell someone that I planned to kill myself the next morning. But I could offer no reason for such a drastic step that would make sense to anyone else. To others, I had simply lost my employment and was struggling to regain it. In my own mind, it was much more than that. My very life and identity had been taken, and I was finding it impossible to regain them. I could no longer exist with the constant frustration of trying to put the pieces back together the way they were before I found myself lying flat on my back at the bottom once more of the employment staircase, looking up at a grueling climb that I couldn't seem to find the strength to make again.

That evening at prayer meeting, I didn't request prayer for myself, not even as a silent request. It was too late for that. How did I manage to hide my deep desire for death in such a place where there was so much support? After prayer meeting ended, my wife Brenda had choir practice. Our two sons were off playing with other kids, so I hid out in the church library, which was no bigger than a walk-in closet. A fellow church member stuck his head into the library.

"Hey, how's it going?" he asked casually. "Have you seen my kids?"

I never actually answered his second question. In fact, my reply rather shocked me. "Not good. Not good at all."

This was the first time I'd admitted to anyone I was in really bad shape. But my fellow church member showed no particular reaction, simply commenting casually, "It'll get better."

His head disappeared, and I was alone again. Perhaps I should have followed him and made it clear this was not an "it'll get better" situation. But I was too far gone for that. I chose to stay alone with my now-gelling suicidal thoughts. After all, no one could change anything. They could only tell me it would get better. And, yes, tomorrow would get better because I would be dead, and that would be far better than hopeless.

I don't remember if I slept much that night or not. I probably did. The thought of ending this mental turmoil was peaceful in comparison to struggling through another day of stress and frustration. The next morning, I got up and headed as usual to the office building I'd come to abhor so deeply in downtown Springfield, Illinois. All I had to do was make sure my normal work routine that morning was nothing out of the ordinary, then drive away and never look back.

So why did I even bother driving to work where I would have to convince my co-workers I was okay? Did I subconsciously want someone to intervene?

As I approached the entrance to my current workplace, I could see nearby the office building where I'd enjoyed so much success before the company merger that had left me to start all over again six years earlier. Did the tantalizing physical proximity of the two office buildings play into my "*so close, yet so far away*" brooding over my inability to regain the life and identity I'd once enjoyed?

I hesitated, vacillating over whether to simply head back to the car and proceed with last night's plan to escape this frustrating existence. Somehow, I pulled myself together enough to make it to my desk. That's where any semblance of normalcy came to an abrupt halt. I froze. I don't think I even blinked that morning. I just stared. I was breathing strangely too.

One co-worker, Linda, had clearly noticed my hyperventilating. She called over the cubical wall to suggest humorously, "Hey, I'm going to buy you some balloons and put all that blowing to good use!"

I didn't reply. The phone rang, jolting me out of my trance. I didn't want to answer, but that would make my co-workers wonder why I ignored it. The call was to confirm a presentation I was scheduled to make that afternoon regarding a new product. The problem was that this particular product was never intended to do what we were being asked to accomplish with it. I have enough trouble presenting something that does work well. I wasn't about to present a product I knew to be the wrong tool for the job. To make matters worse, that was about all I did know concerning this product.

As I hung up the phone, full-blown panic set in. I decided it was time. I stuffed my pockets with small rubber bands, plastic bags, and tape. I then told a co-worker I was going to lunch, taking care to make it sound like I'd be back. I made the short walk to my car, but once inside, I just sat there, staring straight ahead and breathing heavily. I remained frozen in the parking lot for my entire lunch hour. A good ten minutes after I was scheduled to have started my presentation, I came to myself enough to think, *they're probably wondering where I am.*

Another twenty minutes passed. I watched people going about their normal day. A sound of laughter really bothered me. I wanted so badly to be able to laugh, even to be able to smile, without it being a mask to hide my despair. As it had done for so many sleepless nights, my mind channel-surfed from one random thought to another. *I can't go back into work. I can't go home. I can't stay here much longer. I can't live like this anymore.*

My "I can't" thoughts eventually gave way to *I don't want anyone I know to find me.* Then, *just drive away and disappear!*

My brief consideration of disappearing to some new place vs. taking my own life was drowned out by a train whistle. Instantly, I yearned to find myself on the tracks in front of that approaching behemoth. This was not a new thought. I hadn't eaten lunch on a workday for quite some time, but had spent the lunch hour in my car, battling similar thoughts. Typically, I would tune into Christian radio to let the Christian music and programming give me enough inspiration to keep trying. But not today. Today the radio was off. I had no fight left in me. All I wanted was to die.

Turning the car engine on, I pulled out of the parking lot. I had no particular destination in mind except away from Springfield and as remote as possible. But I'd finally and firmly resolved where I *wasn't* going—back to my existence that could no longer be called a life. I exited onto a one-way street that led out of Springfield towards the east. Since my only thought was to head out of town, I have no idea why I didn't simply continue onto I-72 and keep driving east. But for no reason whatsoever, I found myself instead on I-55, heading north.

This route took me past the town of Lincoln, Illinois. Not once did I think about my friend Ed, who worked there and would have gladly helped me. He later told me that he was really mad at me for being so close and not seeking him out. After his initial shock wore off, he clarified that he understood my mind wasn't working properly that day.

In actuality, if my mind had been working properly, I'd have headed south. Since my goal was to find a remote area, I would come across far more such in southern Illinois' Shawnee National Forest than off I-55 north out of Springfield. But I'd found decision-making difficult for quite some time now. My wife Brenda had picked up on this, but she just thought I was being even slower in the morning than my usual non-morning-person self.

I was still thinking remote as I drove north, but could not make the decision to exit the highway. If I didn't exit soon, I'd end up in Chicago. I definitely didn't want to go there, so I started making random exits and turns without noting the roads or directions.

Then I found it. I was on a narrow road in the middle of nowhere. On both sides of the road, corn stalks stood tall. To my right between the road and cornfield was a large, empty arc of gravel. This was as remote as it was going to get between Springfield and Chicago.

I pulled off the road and came to a stop, relieved that it was just about over. I stretched and tugged several small rubber bands down over my head and around my neck. They didn't cut off my breathing as much as I thought they would. I added several more, hoping that all together they would cut off my airway. But breathing still came too easily. This wasn't going to work. A plastic bag would, though, especially if I used some tape or more rubber bands.

Then my worst fear materialized. A car pulled in. I laid my seat back, adjusted my coat to hide the rubber bands, and pretended to be asleep. There was nothing here. Whoever had stopped would likely just get out, stretch their legs, and then leave. But by the time the first car left, another car had pulled in.

This can't be happening! I told myself.

I would just need to wait for the second car to leave. By this time the rubber bands had tightened around my neck and were making me feel lightheaded. I prayed for death. More random thoughts jumped around in my head. *They're really wondering where I am now! Is anyone at work concerned about me? They're probably mad at me for missing the presentation. Would anyone notice if I put a plastic bag over my head?*

Just then I heard footsteps right next to my car. No, I'd better not try the plastic bag. I didn't want someone noticing it and calling the police. I started to shake and cry. I sobbed out, "Go away! Go away! Go away!"

But as nearly three hours passed, I was never there alone. Between the heat from the sun beating through my closed car windows and the coat I was wearing, as well as the tightness of the rubber bands around my neck and lack of fresh air, I should have fallen unconscious. I became concerned that the length of time I'd been there would draw attention. My teal Grand Am didn't exactly blend in with the cornfield.

I had to find another location, but first I had to get clearheaded enough to drive. I tried to remove the rubber bands, but by now they were so tight and my neck so swollen I couldn't get my fingers under them. "Great! How am I going to get these off?"

Then I remembered the keychain pocket knife that each father in our church had received a few months earlier in celebration of Father's Day. It was hanging on my key-ring. I looked at the two-inch by one-inch silver oblong with its black rectangular inset that spelled out the church name and phone number. A pair of scissors opened up on one edge, a one-and-a-quarter-inch-long blade on the other. I opened the blade, debating whether to cut the rubber bands or myself.

I slid the flat part of the blade along my neck, then turned the sharp edge toward the rubber bands. SNAP, they were off! Now it was decision time. Should I continue as planned and get further away from Springfield? Or go back to a lot of angry, confused people? Even as I recognized that this small keepsake may have saved my life, I still couldn't make myself turn to the church, my family, or God. But if I went back home, there'd be no more hiding my condition.

More thoughts raced through my already frazzled mind. *I simply can't go home. I need help they can't give. I don't want to be admitted to the hospital. Maybe the psychiatrist I'd seen for my panic attacks could help me.*

Taking a deep breath, I sat up and looked at myself in the rearview mirror. There were red dots all around my reddened eyes. I later learned this was petechial hemorrhaging from lack of oxygen. My neck was covered with ligature marks. While the strangulation had not proved fatal, these were all clear signs of a serious attempt.

An hour after I cut the rubber bands, my head began to clear. I decided to go back Springfield and talk to my psychiatrist or someone, anyone, at the Southern Illinois University (SIU) School of Medicine psychiatry office. Maybe this wasn't the right place to go, but it was the only one I was familiar with that had people trained to handle such a situation and who could possibly do something for me that did not involve hospitalization.

But even as I prepared to head back, one problem loomed very large. I'd gotten intentionally lost and had a very poor sense of direction. Nor did I have GPS in the car or any other means of retracing my route. How would I find my way back? Since I wasn't particularly anxious to make it back, I silently wished to be in a fatal car accident. One that would result in just my own death with no one else getting hurt. Strange as it may sound, I was more concerned at that moment about the physical lives of any strangers if I got into an accident than the emotional pain of the people who loved me.

God's plan for me was clearly to make it back before the SIU psychiatry office closed, because He not only didn't allow me to be in a car accident, He didn't even allow me to make a single wrong turn. I pulled safely into the tiny parking lot, then walked snail-slow across to the SIU entrance. Every fiber of my being wanted to run back to the car. In fact, I'd left my car door hanging open, though not intentionally. In my state of mind, it was a wonder I even turned the engine off. It was just like getting to my desk that morning all over again. With each step I had to decide whether to take the next or back out while I still could. I could feel another freeze-up coming on.

When I reached the reception desk, the receptionist looked up at me. "May I help you?"

I just stood there, an awkward silence filling the room.

She continued, "Are you ok?"

"I . . . I—" Slowly, I forced the words out, a sustained pause between each one. *Do I really want to tell her this?* "I . . . tried . . . to . . . kill . . . myself . . . today."

Spiritual Application

It's easy to say we believe that God's ways are higher than our ways and that His thoughts are higher than our thoughts. But it is when God's thoughts and ways create havoc with our life and future plans that we question the truth of that statement. We must believe strongly that everything God does is for our good and His glory. Until we reach this conclusion, we will question God every time His plans don't align with ours. And that happens more often than we might like to admit.

In my own case, years of hard-earned employment success had been swept away like a tornado clearing everything in its path. But that was exactly what God knew needed to happen in my life in order for Him to replace my drive for status and material possessions with something far better. He was replacing my plans with His plans. Plans that would ultimately change the desire of my heart from attaining a life of abundance to attaining an abundant life. From attaining earthly success to attaining God's definition of success. I had to be willing to admit the miserable failure of my attempts to recreate what God had allowed to get swept away. Only then would I be ready to embark on a journey to success redefined.

Practical Application

May I urge you, reader, not to make my own mistake. Don't keep problems hidden from the people closest to you. Talk to them. This may cause pain initially, but the longer you keep a problem hidden, the greater this initial pain will be. The worst-case scenario is for your loved ones to find out only after you've taken your own life that you cut off their support when you needed them most. So don't clam up. Don't keep your pain bottled up, trying to buy time to come up with a solution on your own. This is not time bought; it is precious time lost.

And if you are on the receiving end of someone in such a situation, listen, listen, listen! If someone opens up to you or says something that rings of desperation, don't walk away assuming it's nothing major. Ask questions and listen closely, not only to the words, but to the tone. Watch the speaker's body language. If they are in a bad place and you are paying attention, even a seemingly positive response can let you know something is wrong. If nothing else, it may be a signal to at least let someone close to this person know something is going on that may need addressed at a deeper level.

CHAPTER TWO
WAR OF WILLS

Jack and Jill went up the hill to fetch a pail of water.
Jack fell down and broke his crown, and Jill came tumbling
after.
Up Jack got and home did trot as fast as he could caper.
Went to bed to mend his head with vinegar and brown paper.

—Author Unknown

All Jack and Jill needed was a pail of water. But during the simple commission of meeting that need, disaster struck. In the United States at least, most of us no longer fetch water in a pail. Still, we all have our own pails we strive to fill to overflowing with hopes and dreams for our lives.

My own aspirations were simple and self-centered. I was able to get my hands on my bucket of hopes and dreams, but only for a very short time. I'd climbed to the top of the hill to earn it, and I held onto it tight. But God had something different in mind for me that necessitated me letting go of my bucket, the hard-earned contents of which I considered I well deserved. Since I wouldn't let go willingly, God allowed a tumble into my life that would forever separate me from its contents. Though at the time of my tumble all I saw was loss, God actually had something much better in mind to replace my bucket's lost contents. But let me first share my climb up that hill in pursuit of a pail overflowing with what seemed at the time everything I could hope for of success and achievement.

I was born on May 13, 1965, the first child of Herb and Kay Lomelino, residents at that time of Virden, Illinois. From the very start, I experienced something out of my control that would later become a life-changing factor. My hip sockets were not aligned properly. Braces could have easily corrected this. But no one, myself included, noticed the problem until my teens. By then it was too late. Surgery was an option, but at the risk that it might leave me unable walk again. It wasn't hard to choose continuing to live with a comparatively minor deformity over a very real possibility of being permanently crippled.

When I was three, my parents moved twenty-six miles north to Springfield, Illinois. Springfield is by no means a metropolis of non-stop activity. But compared to Virden, where homecoming was the big event of the year, we were headed to the big city.

Springfield itself is located approximately ninety miles northeast of St. Louis, Missouri, and two hundred miles southwest of Chicago, Illinois. While Chicago boasts at least twenty times more people than Springfield and immense political influence, it is not the capital of Illinois as many outsiders mistakenly think. That distinction is held by Springfield, most widely known as the hometown of Abraham Lincoln.

Despite Springfield's historical and political flavor, growing up in Central Illinois' "big town" in the 1970s involved little more than the usual going to school and spending time with friends. My best friend in our early years of grade school was a boy named Tom Pendleton. By 1977, Tom had moved with his family to Bowling Green, Ohio, which is located approximately twenty-five miles south of Toledo, Ohio. There his father, Tom Pendleton, Sr., went into business for himself, establishing Pendleton and Sons Builders. It was in Bowling Green that Tom would in turn become close friends with my future wife Brenda Wickard.

Brenda was born to Jack and Carol Wickard on August 11th, 1965, the youngest of four siblings. She was a spitfire from the start, and I have a picture to prove it. What baby poses with fists clenched and a look on their face that has *I'm going to punch your lights out and enjoy doing it* written all over it? Brenda grew up three miles south of Bowling Green in the tiny town of Portage. With a population of only five hundred, Portage is famous for absolutely nothing. Brenda attended church in nearby Bowling Green at Trinity United Methodist Church, where we would eventually exchange our wedding vows.

My own family was as typical as they came—a dad, a mom, two kids, and a dog. My sister Kim was six years younger, meaning that by the time I was ending my teen years, she was just entering hers. I'm fairly certain that with only two children, my parents hadn't planned to have a teenager in the house for fourteen years straight. Planned or not, they survived our teen years. We grew up attending a church that was equal parts truth and legalism. This soured me on the Christian life and religion in general. It also left me confused about what I believed spiritually and how I wanted to live my life.

Let me make clear that this church did teach a lot of biblical truth. But it also added a lot of extra-biblical rules such as that a male's hair couldn't touch the ears or shirt collar. Going swimming with females was given the name "mixed bathing" to make it sound far worse than it really was. Going to restaurants that served alcohol was considered an appearance of evil.

In my teen years, I strove to prove both the church and my parents wrong about such rules and the many other seemingly-absurd ways in which they were trying to keep me from worldliness and protect me from entering a life of sin. Perhaps the biggest taboo my parents and I battled over was music. One day I purchased an 8-track tape by the rock group Kiss, which was titled *Love Gun*. The cover art showed the band members standing close together in their costumes and white face makeup with beautiful, scantily-clad women stretched out in suggestive poses at their feet, their own face also covered in white makeup. Both the title and cover art left little to the imagination as to the album's subject matter. I did a lousy job of keeping the tape hidden, and before I knew it, Mom and I were back in the store.

The worst part was that I couldn't return the tape for cash. I had to trade it, which left me ending up with John Travolta. His songs probably weren't any more edifying, but Kiss was banned from the Lomelino residence.

Unfortunately, the more something is banned, the more appealing it can become. I spent many days down the street at the house of a friend who was a Kiss fanatic. But my biggest thrill came from listening to contraband Kiss albums at home, literally right under my parent's feet. Having a bedroom in the basement did have its advantages!

One evening, I even managed to lie my way out of the house to attend a Kiss concert. It wasn't so much that I was a huge Kiss fan as that I wanted to see why my parents and so many others hated the group. What made Kiss huge wasn't just the music, volume, and look. Some of it at least was rebellion against parents trying to single out this particular music group as THE enemy in their war against rock and roll. Kiss doesn't call their fans the Kiss army for nothing.

I have to admit my dad did win one very crucial argument over what I felt were ridiculous and unbiblical restrictions on living the Christian life. Of all my teenage skirmishes with my parents, one simple question and one simple answer have stuck with me. I asked my dad, "What if you're wrong?"

A summation of Dad's reply was that if he was wrong he had still lived a good life and given up nothing worth losing his soul over. He then turned the tables, asking me, "What if *you're* wrong?"

My parents may have majored on the minors too often for my liking, thanks in part to what was being taught in our church. But they got right that Jesus was my only hope of a life worth living on this earth and, more importantly, eternal life in Heaven.

By this time, my one goal was to complete high school, then move out from under my parent's rules and never attend church again. I graduated in 1983. Shortly after in early summer, my grade-school friend Tom Pendleton called from Bowling Green to suggest I try to get a job working for his dad's company. If Tom Sr. hired me, I could even live with the Pendletons until I found my own place.

I didn't think twice about distancing myself figuratively as well as 450 miles literally from my past. Why I thought living with my boss was a good idea is beyond me. I must have been too focused on the reunion with my former best friend as well as a chance to live unencumbered by my parents' rules. Good, bad, or otherwise, the plan came together quickly, and I headed off, bound for success and independence in Bowling Green.

At this point God had to be rolling with laughter. My plans and His could not have been more different. I wanted to start a new life that did not include any of the restrictions church had placed on me. Living 450 miles from home would allow me to dump my old life and start over. Sure, it felt strange leaving my home and parents. I loved my parents and always would. But I hated the rules and restrictions, even if they were intended for my good, as much as I loved my family. Right up there with the suffocating rules, I hated attending church three times a week. It would be such a relief to live my own life without my parents constantly questioning my choices.

That my parents knew I was planning to dump everything they had taught me made my sendoff awkward. They also knew there wasn't a thing they could do about it. All they could do was love me and pray God would protect me from myself.

For my part, I pulled out of the driveway with mixed emotions. But by the time I'd driven my 1976 Audi 100LS a few blocks, I was celebrating. That celebration continued all the way to the edge of town. Then God stepped in and showed me He was in control. Just as I was about to pull out onto the highway, my car died. My celebration turned to complete silence.

Though I tried to figure out what was wrong, I could find no apparent reason why the car wouldn't start. It had simply lost power to everything. Not such a surprise, since the car had spent more time, it seemed, in repair shops than on the road. Eventually I had to call my parents to come rescue me. The problem turned out to be an electrical issue. Once it was fixed, I had to spend one more night at home. Worst of all, I had to relive that awkward sendoff all over again. However, with that indestructible mindset teens have, I simply set off again in the same undependable car. The Audi did get me to Bowling Green, though I found driving 450 miles a lot less fun and more stressful in a car that had so recently left me stranded.

Despite my slight delay, I arrived in Bowling Green thinking that now *my* plans had at last begun. But God's plan had never changed. It was still playing out in His perfect time. God knew I would need a lot of help down the road, and that help showed up on my first day in Bowling Green when Tom took me to the local K-mart. There he introduced me to a good friend of his from school days who worked in the sporting goods department—Brenda Wickard, my future wife.

I will be honest that it was not love at first sight, since my focus at that time was totally on myself and the new life that in my mind I alone controlled. In actuality, as God had made clear in the message He sent me when my car died at the edge of Springfield, **He** alone was in control of my life. But God would have to teach me many more lessons before that message would make sense.

As arranged, I began work at Pendleton and Sons Builders. But it took me only a few days to recognize the huge difference between the demands of an actual paying job and vocational school, which I had attended half-days during my junior and senior years of high school. Here I was, a skinny kid with little muscle, trying to keep pace with brawny home remodelers who could carry multiple bundles of shingles up a ladder.

Not only did I quickly discover I didn't have the proper body for this type of work, but that I lacked the necessary skills as well. My employer, Tom Sr., informed me that I was better at tearing things up than putting them together. This led to my assignment to help remove old roofing and other building materials, then haul the debris to the dump. That sounded simple enough. Only I couldn't drive the stick-shift van without killing it. Nor could I back up the trailer without jackknifing it. As to the roofing itself, I discovered that slate was both sharp and slippery, a bad combination on a sloped roof.

My gofer abilities—go for this, go for that—proved just as poor. Tom Sr. learned for certain we weren't on the same page when he sent me to buy four five-pound boxes of 16-penny nails. I returned with five one-pound boxes of nails. In my mind, I'd heard *four or five pound* boxes of 16-penny nails. That anyone would buy twenty entire pounds of nails at one time hadn't even occurred to me. Somehow, I survived an entire pay period and received my first paycheck. If I knew then what I know now, I would have put most of that away for getting my own place. Instead, I blew my paycheck on a car stereo.

At this point, I found myself still living in someone else's house and still stuck following someone else's rules. I was also still attending church. This was because the Pendletons attended church. To be specific, Trinity United Methodist Church, the same church where Brenda Wickard attended. But the new Steven didn't bother focusing on the sermons. I was far too focused on the females for that.

Then on October 28, 1983, Trinity held a youth group costume party lock-in. This means that the youth group was *locked in* the church overnight. Neither Brenda nor I were particularly interested in attending, Brenda because her grandmother had recently died and she didn't feel like partying, myself because I wasn't big on getting together with a bunch of church kids. But we'd both been talked into it.

This was the first real encounter between Brenda and I beyond that casual introduction at K-mart, and our conversation started out a bit awkward. Brenda wore an eye-catching high school class ring. I asked if I could see it. The ring was engraved *"BOWLING GREEN HIGH Class of 83 BRENDA"*. I had obviously left at home the filter between my brain and mouth since I immediately blurted out, "No way! You're too old to have just graduated!"

Smooth, huh? Brenda let the insult slide. Somehow we moved into the subject of music. She told me her favorite artist was Pat Benatar, an American female rock singer popular in the 1980s. Since I had just bought Pat's new release *Live from Earth* and a new car stereo, this was an opportunity even I couldn't mess up. We were soon in my car, listening to Pat. I sometimes tell people Pat Benatar brought Brenda and I together. It's sort of true.

Of course since this was a lock-**in,** we eventually had to go back **in** the church. We stretched out amongst the other teens scattered across the basement floor, our eyes locked on each other, saying nothing, but knowing a connection had been made. *My parents' church would sure never have allowed any of this!* I thought to myself.

Considering that our brief introduction at K-mart and the lock-in were the only occasions Brenda and I had spent together, it must have been immediately obvious that I had it bad for her. Maybe it wasn't love at first sight, but it was definitely love at second sight. When I got back to the Pendletons the next morning, Tom's younger brother Neil, who'd been at the lock-in, facetiously asked me, "How many *minutes* have you known her?"

Those scant minutes soon turned out to be very precious. The busy remodeling season would soon end when full winter set in, and I was falling far short of Tom, Sr.'s expectations. He did me a huge favor by letting me know before I signed my apartment lease that he wasn't going to keep me on. At this point, I was only a week into my relationship with Brenda and far more concerned about losing her than losing my job. In that short time, we'd both recognized we were meant to be together. How the girl could actually fall asleep during a James Bond movie might be an unfathomable mystery. But I knew Brenda was the only one for me, and the feeling was clearly mutual.

Unfortunately, Tom, Sr. was sending me back to Springfield to "grow up". Our whirlwind week of falling in love would soon turn into a heart-wrenching long-distance relationship for Brenda and me, separated by four hundred and fifty miles of Ohio, Indiana, and Illinois highways. Still, we had one last unforgettable date before that happened. I don't remember a thing about our time inside the Red Lobster restaurant. It's what happened when we tried to leave that makes that evening unforgettable.

My car had just cleared the restaurant parking lot when the lights and sirens of three Ohio State police vehicles came on. They immediately pulled me over. Brenda and I were ordered to exit our vehicle and put our hands on the roof. I'll never forget the two of us looking at each other across the roof of my car. I was wondering, *who did I get involved with?* We were both having trouble processing what was happening, and the police weren't explaining their actions while still in the process of their investigation.

The whole scene was surreal. There were the three police cars with lights flashing. Police with drawn guns were telling us to put our hands back on the roof if we lifted them more than an inch. The officers gave us a pat-down, then searched the car. This lasted for a long time because what they were looking for did not exist.

Here's what had actually happened. While packing for my return to Springfield, I had slid a large, but legal knife onto my belt. I'd thought nothing further of it until we were halfway across the Red Lobster parking lot. Turning to Brenda, I'd indicated the knife. "This is going to look real cute in there!"

I decided it would be wise to leave the knife in the car. Brenda went on inside while I headed back, removing the knife from my belt as I walked to the car. I stored the knife in the glove box, then joined Brenda inside. A rookie police officer had witnessed the episode, but had mistaken my knife for a gun. Combined with my out-of-state license plates, the error had led to quite a fiasco.

"Could this be what you saw?" one of the officers asked the rookie, holding up the knife. He admitted it must have been since their thorough search had turned up nothing else. Brenda and I were given a half-explanation, half-apology, then allowed to go on our way. By that time, I was definitely ready to get out of Ohio.

Our two families were quick to tell Brenda and me not to expect a one-week relationship to last. They were sure one of us would decide a long-distance relationship was too difficult. Brenda wrote *I Love Steve* on her dresser mirror. Her older sister, Deb, wrote *Really?* We still have that dresser. Deb's *Really?* and Brenda's confident *yep* have faded during our three decades together. *I Love Steve* is still there, and she still does. Other little love notes to each other cover the remainder of the mirror. As a mirror, it is of little good. As a reminder, it is priceless.

Still, our long-distance relationship wasn't easy. I dated other girls occasionally, but nothing clicked as it had with Brenda. Our parents were gracious about their phone bills. We talked often, but our main form of communication was handwritten letters. The calls and letters helped us get to know each other on a deeper level. We couldn't just sit silently in a movie theater for a couple hours and call it time spent together. We had to actually communicate.

When I had the chance, I would drive to Brenda's home in Portage, Ohio. It wasn't long before I had the entire eight-hour route memorized: I-72 E to I-57 N to I-74 E to I-465 S to I-70 E to I-75 N. I could recite it backwards as well, but I won't bother. I didn't care much for that direction.

One trip in particular stands out from all the others. Brenda had time off, but I didn't. She couldn't afford to fly and wouldn't drive alone. The only way to get her to Springfield was for me to drive to Portage, put her into my car, then head immediately back. I called a couple friends. "Do you want to do something crazy?"

Without hesitation, they both said yes. The three of us spent sixteen hours with little interruption in a Chevette, driving to pick Brenda up and bring her back to Springfield. Chevettes were not built for comfortable long-distance travel, especially for more than one or two people. I'm sure I enjoyed the last eight hours more than my friends did, since I now had my favorite girl with me for the return trip.

There were other in-person visits. But it was mainly phone calls and letters for the twenty-eight months between becoming a couple on October 28th, 1983, and when we were married on February 28, 1986. Thankfully, the large wooden cross suspended above the platform on which we were married decided to wait until March 1, 1986, to fall. After the whole Ohio State Police incident, I'm not sure how I would have taken it had that cross fallen during our wedding ceremony.

Spiritual Application

The statement *you can run but you can't hide* is never truer than when applied to someone trying to run from God. In a futile attempt to overrule God's will with my own, I ran from God's church and from the parents God gave me. But there was no running from Him. Whether or not human beings may get overly zealous with the rules of the Christian life, God is my Creator, and His perfect rules still applied to my life. God was as much in control of my life in Ohio, where I had run away from Christian influence, as He was when I was at home where, if anything, it seemed there was too much Christian influence.

Running from God only accomplishes one thing, and that is to make Him pursue you. God knew I was trying to avoid Him in Ohio. He knows your hiding place as well. From our human perspective, it may seem that God's will is to crush us under the weight of an endless list of rules we can never come close to obeying. Nothing is further from the truth. The crushing rules are man-made. God's rules are freeing and well within our ability. Just listen to what Jesus Himself sums up as being God's most important rules to obey:

Love the LORD your God with all your heart, all your soul, and all your mind. This is the first and greatest commandment. A second is equally important: "Love your neighbor as yourself." The entire law and all the demands of the prophets are based on these two commandments" Matthew 22:37-40 (NLT).

Practical Application

When picking your battles in the war of wills, whether with your teenagers, spouses, or someone else, major on the majors and minor on the minors. Majoring on the minors simply increases in the other person the natural human tendency to oppose authority, which will then spill over even into the major things. It also devalues our emotional currency if we keep making a big deal out of little things. As result, when we do make a big deal out of a big deal—i.e., major on the majors—we will be seen as making more out of an issue than is there because that is the pattern we have established.

CHAPTER THREE
SUCCESS

S uccess. It's hardly first on a list of reasons for attempting suicide. But that's how it started for me. I was in the right place at the right time with the right people opening the right doors. Sure, I had discovered that home remodeling was not going to be my life's work. But my time in Ohio had proved an adventure, and I'd also met my future wife, so it didn't at all fall in the complete failure category. Failure would come much later. By the time it did, I had experienced so many years of easy success that I had no idea how to properly respond to it.

I returned home in late fall of 1983 with no job and the knowledge that construction of any sort wasn't a good career option for me. So I enrolled in an electronics program at Lincoln Land Community College. On the career-path side of things, I also attempted to enroll in the Illinois Air National Guard, whose 183rd fighter wing is located on the north end of Springfield.

This is when my life-long issue of misaligned hip sockets changed the course of my life. I was turned away without hesitation as soon as they noticed my left leg with its foot going to the left and knee going to the right simultaneously. That my right leg had a similar, if less pronounced, issue didn't help my case. I made a mild attempt to explain that I had compensated adequately for this problem my entire life. But concerned about future medical liability, the Illinois Air National Guard sent me on my way.

Around this time, a friend of the family, Charles Proctor, put in a good word in for me with his own employer, Central Illinois Public Service (CIPS), a Springfield-based utility company that serviced most of downstate Illinois. I was hired by CIPS in 1984 as a part-time janitor-slash-security guard at the Illinois building, starting literally at the bottom in location as well as position and pay. Along with the first floor lobby, I spent much of my time in the basement and sub-basement. I did my best to avoid one particular elevator. Every time it reached the sub-basement, it would announce, "Lower level going DOWN." Since the sub-basement was supposed to **be** the lowest level, this gave me a horror-movie chill the first time I heard it. I knew the elevator would always go up, but I still didn't like hearing that ominous statement.

Once I completed the cleaning part of my janitorial duties, which only took about two hours of an eight-hour shift, my job involved sitting in the lobby for hours on end. CIPS calling this the security guard portion of my part-time position was just a clever way to say that when no one else was there, I would be—nights, weekends, holidays. That's when I realized I was not the low man on the totem pole. I was in the ground below the low man on the totem pole. For a guy just out of high school, though, it was still sweet. There were times when I had seventeen floors all to myself. As I looked out over Springfield from the top of the building, I would think about how many 18-year-old kids were sweating for a paycheck at fast food restaurants or behind a lawn mower.

During the work week, one of my main jobs entailed retrieving cars belonging to upper management from the sub-basement. The basement itself had an underground parking garage with a ramp going down into it from the street level. The company president, vice-presidents, and other members of upper management preferred, of course, to park their big, expensive cars there out of the elements, especially since the underground garage was much closer than the company parking lot.

All the cars didn't fit in the basement garage, so some had to be moved down to the sub-basement. This could only be accessed by the stairs, regular elevator, and the freight or, as we called it, the car elevator. Management's luxury cars fit into the freight elevator, but with little room to spare. This made moving them from one level to the other a bit nerve-racking. Since the car owners weren't about to do this, it fell into the part-time janitor's job description to hustle down when one of the managers needed his car parked in the sub-basement or brought up for him when he left.

The security guard part of my job didn't match up with the title very well at all. It was far less any actual security surveillance than just getting the people who belonged in the building inside and keeping the people who didn't belong there out. Since there were entrances on both the ground floor and the basement, I spent a lot of time running up and down stairs between the two levels to open either the front door or the parking garage door at the bottom of the ramp.

On weekends and holidays, my so-called janitorial position consisted even more so of the security aspect. On those days, most of my time was spent in the lobby so I could let people in after the doors were locked to the public. At a utility company there was always the possibility of an employee having to come in to address some time-sensitive matter during the wee hours of the morning. But I was essentially getting paid to do my college homework, play solitaire, and write love letters to Brenda. This was all permissible. Sleeping on the job was the only thing that wasn't permissible. Though when you have an 11 PM to 7 AM shift with only a few hours' worth of work to do, that's still going to happen sometimes.

The people for whom I typically opened the door after normal business hours were computer programmers, computer operators, and computer room supervisors. Getting to know the people who went in and out of the computer room 24/7 hastened my advancement. They would stop and talk to me about my classes and career goals. They saw me probably more than they wanted to. Nothing to do with me, but because any time the computer room staff were called in outside of regular work hours, it meant something had gone awry in the tenth floor computer room.

This was back in the dark ages of computing when room-sized mainframes with reel-to-reel tape drives ran COBOL programs. I knew nothing about mainframe computers, and there were no classes on it other than COBOL programming. I was literally opening the door for them, but getting to know them was figuratively opening the door for me to enter their world. I tried to find out why the mainframe was on the tenth floor or how they got that huge, heavy thing up there in the first place, but I never did get a good answer. I avoided the ninth floor as much as possible because I was concerned the mainframe might just come crashing down through the ceiling on top of me.

In 1987, a few months after Brenda and I were married, I was promoted to full-time janitor. The promotions continued in quick succession to courier in 1988, then to computer operator in 1989. The next flight up on the CIPS employment staircase took me in 1991 to production control, specifically, data control clerk.

Production control was made up of three positions: scheduler, endeavor specialist, and data control clerk. When I was offered the production control position, I was told that none of the applicants had met all of the necessary requirements. The company wanted to promote from within. They were aware of my excellent performance in the electronics classes I'd been taking back when I was a janitor. Since I'd also proven myself as a quality employee in the entry level computer operator position, they felt that with proper training I would quickly catch on to the responsibilities of the data control clerk.

The catch was that within six months I would have to meet the required job qualifications. And I would have to do this with only on-the-job training. If I failed, since my prior job would already be filled, I could end up being let go and have nothing. My own conclusion was that everything I'd done prior to this had proved successful, so why not go for it. After all, if management didn't think I could do this, they wouldn't have offered me the position. It was a risk I was willing to take, and once again success came easily.

As the data control clerk, I was responsible for setting up the nightly batch of processing. Any computer code that changed on a regular basis was my responsibility: dates, check numbers, stock rates, and many other variables. This was about 10% of the job. The other 90% was catering to the programmers and end users. But it was the 10% that was most critical. This information was either 100% right or 100% wrong. A single misplaced period or comma would cause a phone call from the night shift, telling me a job had abnormally ended. In CIPS computer lingo, this was called an "abend".

When I walked the computer room staff through a problem while lying in bed next to Brenda, she would tell me, "I'm glad they understood what you just said because I didn't get any of it!"

Most of the time, those phone calls were easy enough to deal with and all in a day's work. Being on-call wasn't much fun, but it gave me a sense of importance, especially since it provided me with my own mobile phone. Since at this time few people had personal cell phones, if you were carrying around a big-as-a-brick communication device, people couldn't help but notice. Others may not have been impressed, but I know my mom was. Her new nickname for me was Dr. Steven.

Other than Brenda losing her job as an office assistant due to owner embezzlement, life was good to us in the late 1980s and early 1990s. In 1989, shortly after the birth of our firstborn Jordan, Brenda and I began attending an excellent area church. By the end of that year, I had come to a personal realization that I needed Jesus Christ as my Savior. I repented of my sin and asked His forgiveness. It is amazing how much bringing a new life into the world had changed me. But this was the beginning of my spiritual journey, and I would have much growing to do before I would submit to Jesus as my **Lord** as well as my Savior.

My parents had started attending the same church once they realized that the legalistic stance of the church in which I'd spent my teen years had only driven me away from faith in Jesus Christ. Our new church proved much more welcoming, even though I will admit I was probably a bit of a pain myself sometimes while going through my own spiritual growing pains.

On September 25th, 1992, our second son, Shaun, was born to us. My own increased income more than made up for Brenda's 1993 employment setback. Life was good.

Only three months into my six-month probation period as data control clerk, I received notice that the job was officially mine. Being somewhat of a perfectionist, I was very good at this job. The all-right or not-right-at-all part didn't bother me too much. I loved calling the payroll department for verification when something didn't look right. *One less abend to deal with tonight,* I would think as I mentally patted myself on the back. The best part, though, was when the payroll supervisor called to sing my praises. This was heady stuff for a man in his mid-twenties.

All this did not come without challenges, though. Some nights I could not shut my mind off. I would go through the check list again and again and again. In the middle of the night, I would be verifying job code I'd already verified that day. What had I missed? Sometimes I felt such high anxiety that I would call work in the middle of the night to check on things. Ninety-nine percent of the time, everything was fine. In essence, I was doing my day's work all over again instead of sleeping.

My co-workers and supervisors saw me as competent and confident. At worst, they saw me as over-conscientious. I could not let them know I was a nervous wreck. I wish now I had admitted my anxiety. A supervisor can't help you with an issue they don't know about.

I began bringing the job code home with me to avoid having to call in. If I could see the code was right, I figured it would alleviate my anxiety. I no longer made verification calls, but my anxiety grew worse. I would awake with a start in the middle of the night, imagining the worst. *I have to check the code*, I'd tell myself.

Brenda caught me a couple of times. I tried to make it sound like I was fine, just doing a quick check so I'd sleep better. Knowing her as I do now, I'm surprised she didn't come right out and call me a liar. She certainly knew what I was up to. Even when I quadruple-checked everything, I still couldn't sleep.

"It's just a computer program," Brenda told me. "If it's wrong, it will get corrected. It's not brain surgery. No one's going to die."

Sleep deprivation and panic attacks soon got the better of me. I was so concerned about getting everything one-hundred percent right that I would have one-hundred percent of the more complex code right, but made stupid mistakes on the easy code. My boss caught on and sat me down. He told me simply, "You know what you're doing. You just need to calm down and do it."

I didn't mind taking a call in the middle of the night to fix a mistake, be it mine or another's. But I could not bear to have someone else called to fix **my** mistake. I knew the programmers would see it as part of their job, and I had a good relationship with most of them. They knew my work ethic and knew human errors, theirs and mine, were inevitable. I always owned up to my mistakes, but my pride didn't like it one bit.

Then it finally happened. I left work at work, had a good evening at home, and got a good night's sleep. The next morning I went to work, sure all was well, only to find a programmer waiting at my desk. She told me I had the executive payroll messed up worse than she had thought was possible. We would have to re-run it during the day, and their pay would be delayed.

I don't know exactly what I responded. But the general gist was, "Well, there isn't anything worse to mess up than the executive payroll, so I might as well stop worrying and do my job the best I can."

I began to learn the other two production control positions and eventually knew enough about them to provide backup to those two personnel. We were equal in capability, but not in pay classification. They had level 13 and 14 supervisory pay grades. I was doing almost the same job for level 5 clerk (C5) pay. I decided to talk to my supervisor, George, about this. I told him that data control clerk was not a C5 position. His response still ranks among the best compliments I have ever received. "It was before you got your hands on it."

No previous data control clerk had put the extra effort in to learn both the other production control positions or learn job code well enough to fix abends that would normally require a programmer or go above and beyond to "spoil" the end users. George put a request in to have the position bumped up to a C11 pay grade. This was no ordinary raise. My hourly pay jumped from $11 to nearly $17. This was the early 1990s. I was in my late twenties with a loving wife and two sons. Now I had the means to correct our past financial mistakes, mainly credit card abuse, and live the American dream with them. Ah, sweet success.

Spiritual Application

Material blessings are not indicators of a life lived for God. Nor is the lack of material blessings indicators of a life lived for self. I was so materially blessed during a time of living for myself. Sure, I had returned to church, but it was still all about me. Attending church kept peace in the family. I felt like a better person. I could and did ask questions that made Sunday School teachers cringe. I had decided to tithe, not as a cheerful giver, but so that I would no longer feel bad when tithing was the sermon topic. Nor would I have to look away as the offering plate passed by.

While my tithe at that time may have helped support our church, my attitude was so displeasing to God that He eventually chose to take away the material blessings. It has become clear to me that God prefers that I tithe out of less with the right attitude than tithe out of more with an attitude of what a great person I've become. God doesn't need our money or want it when we are doing it for our own glory or for any other misplaced reason. God wants our willing, loving obedience in this and all other areas of our lives.

Practical Application

Spend less than you make, including the tithe, and save the rest. Tithing a minimum of 10%, saving 10%, and living on the rest is a good starting point. The earlier you start, the easier this is. After leaving home and starting a family, it becomes increasingly more difficult. I had a great income and lived as though it would only continue to increase. I lived above my means because I wanted to have and do more than my income allowed. The combination of over-spending and under-saving created major financial problems when our income drastically decreased. It would have still been a big adjustment if we'd been saving properly, but we would have been in a far better financial position to deal with it.

Also, don't purchase anything on credit that you can't immediately pay off or that is non-essential. I was taught little about money. Brenda too grew up in a do-what-you-want-when-you-want, figure-out-later-how-to-pay-for it environment. One of the first things I bought on a credit card was a large teddy bear at an amusement park. When the bottom dropped out, I still owed money on that credit card. I paid interest on top of interest on that teddy bear for so long that I dubbed it the world's most expensive teddy bear. You overpay for anything purchased on credit that you can't quickly pay off, no matter how good of a deal it looks like on the front end.

CHAPTER FOUR
IF I, THEN GOD

With my new promotion and C11 pay grade, I was on top of the world. But just two weeks later, my attainment of the American dream became the source of a real life nightmare. It started with the announcement that natural gas and electricity providers Central Illinois Public Service (CIPS) and Union Electric (UE), based in St. Louis, Missouri, were merging into a new company that would eventually be called Ameren. It was called a merger of equals, but a pessimistic co-worker immediately began referring to CIPS as "UE North", since what resulted seemed far more a takeover by the Missouri-based UE than any actual pooling of resources and personnel.

A few months later, my co-worker was proven right when most of the CIPS Information Technology (IT) staff were forced to look for work elsewhere. The people leading the merger initiative clearly had a much different definition of *equal* than those people the merger caused to lose their jobs. For me, the timing of finding my niche and the CIPS/UE merger could not have been worse. I knew it was nothing personal and that I hadn't really failed at CIPS. But that didn't make it any easier to wrap my mind around the fact that what had taken me fourteen years to attain had lasted only two weeks after my promotion finally made me equal with the two others I'd supported.

Ironically, when I received my pay grade change at CIPS was when I first thought that I should start tithing. After all, with just a simple okay from payroll to my supervisor's request on my behalf, my pay had increased nearly six dollars an hour. Sure, it would have shown a lot more living by faith if I'd decided to tithe before my promotion. But I figured God would still give me credit for tithing, period.

Of course I had no idea how temporary my newfound wage would be when I made the decision to tithe. If I'd known what was coming, still being an infant in the faith, I'm sure I would have continued to put off tithing as part of my Christian life.

However, I had heard a particular story many times. And I'd experienced a variety of responses to it. I'd believed it, but not enough to take action. I'd felt mixed emotions. I'd had the frustrated thought, *Why doesn't anything like that ever happen to me?*

This time I bought all the way in. But it wasn't faith in God, come what may. It was more an attempt to stay on God's good side in hopes of avoiding financial disaster. Here is the simplest version of the story in question.

"Once upon a time . . . a family was struggling to make ends meet. The bank was about to foreclose on them. There wasn't enough money to make both the house payment and tithe. The family saw this as a test of faith, so they trusted God and continued to tithe. The next day they discovered an anonymous source had given them more than enough money to make the house payment . . . and they all lived happily ever after."

Obviously, the story isn't typically told with the fairy tale beginning and ending. It is a fairy tale, nonetheless, even if it really did happen to someone, because it is told to make you believe that if you have the same faith in God, money will miraculously fall out of the sky for you too. Better yet, God will not only cover the house payment, but will cover everything else too. Trust God with the tithe, and He will provide, no sacrifice required.

Problem was, at this time I didn't realize it was a fairy tale. So I bought into it. When talk of the merger first started, I wasn't completely shocked. After all, I'd been taught that the more we do what is right, the more Satan brings things into our lives to discourage us. So I dug in deeper, resolved to trust God to provide.

Then rumor gave way to an official announcement that the IT department would relocate to St. Louis. Still resolute, I was ready to move my family and anxious to see how God would provide in response to our acceptance of His will in this unseen change. Then came the announcement that Ameren didn't need two IT departments. The new merged department would consist largely of IT personnel already in St. Louis along with a select few from CIPS. I soon learned that I was not one of the transfers.

I prayed, trusting that God would show me what to do. God had to lead. God had to provide. That's how the story always ends. That was all I had left to hold onto. "God, I need you to intervene now," I pleaded, "or my story is going to end with Steven chose to trust God, and he lost everything!"

God had given me the ability to work my way up at CIPS, blessing me with promotion after promotion. I could not continue to trust in my income and credit cards. But I did believe wholeheartedly that if I tithed, then God would continue to bless me monetarily.

Unfortunately, that mentality was totally unbiblical. Jesus didn't want me to trust Him for my success, financial or otherwise. He wanted me to trust Him in all circumstances. That sounds so simple, but it is not. God's definition of success and mine are so radically different that it is hard for me to get a mental grasp on it. However, when the merger sent me next to a completely new position, I didn't understand that. Since I didn't lose my pay, I figured continuing to tithe would keep me in God's good graces, at which point an "if I, then God" mentality took hold.

Spiritual Application

Forgiving the people, or in my case the companies, behind injustice is only part of the process of getting beyond injustice. The hard part of the process is forgiving injustice itself. The reality is that we live in a world plagued by injustice, and every one of us will experience injustice repeatedly one way or another. To truly believe that God works all things together for our good, we have to believe that God can work through injustice for our good. If we never come to terms with past and/or present injustice, it becomes unnecessary baggage we will drag around throughout our entire life. The inability to forgive injustice can also lead to a broken relationship with God for allowing the injustice to happen.

Practical Application

The only constant in this life is change. If life is going great, don't expect it to stay that way. If life is going awful, don't expect it to stay that way. Life is totally unpredictable, so don't get caught thinking life can't get better or can't get worse, because it will.

CHAPTER FIVE
THE LIFE RAFT:
EMPLOYMENT HELL YEAR 1

T o replace local offices for customer service, the CIPS/UE merger, now called Ameren, created a new entity, the Pawnee Call Center, which was a half-hour commute from Springfield in Pawnee, Illinois. Small-town southern Illinois customers were used to heading over to their local CIPS office, where they could do business and chat with people they actually knew. So they absolutely hated Ameren's decision to close all the local offices, replacing them with a distant call center full of strangers.

I was just as unenthusiastic. Fourteen years of my life had been invested in CIPS, and they now amounted to nothing. My hard-earned production control position was gone. I knew I did not have the special personality it takes to work at a call center, but since the Pawnee Call Center was brand new, they had a lot of positions to fill and were accepting anyone remotely qualified. So I reluctantly accepted a position there as a customer service representative (CSR) for the simple reason that it allowed me to hold on to my hard-earned raise. The merger had taken place over several months, and it was March, 1997, when I began working at the Pawnee Call Center, though it wasn't until December 31, 1997, that CIPS and UE officially became Ameren.

I have a lot of funny stories from my time at the call center, but the job itself and I were a total mismatch. It was all about speed. I was all about accuracy and thoroughness. Still, while I didn't want or like the job, it was the only door God had opened. Though thoroughly confused, I chose contentment and continued to try to put God first in everything. I had decided to honor God in my finances whether I received another promotion or not. To me, the job God provided at the Pawnee Call Center was just another test of my faith. I'd lost the hard-earned job I loved, but at least my income was the same. Would I accept this life raft job as His will for my life and thank Him that I hadn't taken a pay cut? If I passed the test, God would put my life back together. I didn't need a prestigious job. I could learn to love my job as a customer service representative just as much.

Trying to stay hopeful, I focused on the fact that a large company, CIPS, was now combined with an even larger company, UE, and that the combination of the two had created one huge company. In this newly formed mega-company, there had to be another position available to me as good or better than production control clerk. All I had to do was ride it out in the call center life raft until another luxury liner position became available. Still, while I knew the Pawnee Call Center was only a stopgap job that I couldn't do for very long, it ended up being even shorter than I expected.

"You are too nice for this job." That's what I was told in my only Pawnee Call Center performance evaluation.

Too nice? All I'd done was treat customers the way I would want to be treated. I didn't have the authority to cut anybody a deal, so it's not that I was telling anyone they didn't have to pay their bill. If common courtesy is too nice, then I was certainly guilty!

In actuality, as much as I tried to be professional and, in my employer's opinion, too nice, the truth was that being on the phone all day with people taking out their frustration on me regarding the merger, local office closings, and long waits to speak with a real person was more than I could take. Oh, the things I wanted to say, but couldn't!

I remember one customer telling me, "Every time the wind blows in this town, my power goes out."

"It sounds like you need to move," I was tempted to respond, knowing the complaint was a huge exaggeration. But I successfully fought off the urge. Even more annoying was one frequently asked question: "Are you a real person?"

This dismayed me to the point that I wanted to answer, "I'm more like a human punching bag right now, so give me your best shot."

Customers who'd had their electricity disconnected often asked, "Why did *you* turn my electricity off?"

"*I* didn't!" I wanted to tell those customers. "I'm just a poor merger victim who has to listen to you gripe about the meat in your freezer going bad after you didn't pay your bill for six months."

The most common question callers asked was, "Where are you?"

How I would have loved to tell them, "Employment hell, thanks for asking!"

I gained great respect for customer service representatives that year. CSRs are probably surprised these days when they take my call and are treated like an actual human being.

Not every call was bad. There were a lot of turn-on-the-electricity, turn-off-the-electricity, and promise-to-pay calls. Then there were calls that were not the least bit funny at the time, but once the smoke had cleared (literally in one case) without those moments of inane dialogue actually worsening the situation, some humor could be found in recalling the conversation. Here are a few of my favorites.

In Third Place: I title this, "Don't panic when the fire department calls."

Me: "House fire. Send a crew to turn off the utilities."

Dispatcher: "Address?"

Me: "I didn't get it. But it's a small town, and it's the only house on fire."

The dispatcher, rightly, called me out for my misplaced use of humor.

In Second Place: Please note that utility companies providing natural gas and electricity are required to be available 24/7 for emergencies.

Customer: "I need to report a gas leak."

Me: "I see the address you're calling from on my computer screen. I'll send someone right over."

Customer: "That's the wrong address. I noticed the leak last night at about seven o'clock and knew you were closed, so I shut up the house and stayed with a friend."

Again, one of those times I couldn't say what I wanted to say, i.e., "So your house now has fourteen hours of natural gas built up in it, assuming it hasn't blown up yet, and you want me to tell a dispatcher to send someone to it?"

Neither the dispatcher nor I saw the humor in this one at that particular moment.

And the Winner: A lesson for mobile home movers.

Customer: "I need to report a wire down and a gas leak."

Me: "Are you okay? Something pretty bad must have happened to have both these occurring at the same time."

Customer: "It's nothing like that. We were just pulling out a mobile home and forgot that the utilities were still connected."

All to say, I've learned great respect for utility dispatchers and their crews. Of course throughout any normal day at PCC, I received only a handful of bad calls. But those and my general dislike of the job were enough to make each day a bad day in my mind. I knew God had provided me with this particular job, so I tried to maintain a proper perspective. I read Christian magazines during lunch and listened to Christian music during my half-hour commute.

My favorite soundtrack that year was the Scott Kripayne CD *Wild Imagination,* which has the song "Sometimes He Calms the Storm". I knew God would eventually calm this storm. What I did not know was that a storm I thought I'd endured to the end had in actuality only just begun. In fact, it was about to get much worse. It is good that God doesn't let us know such disheartening facts in advance.

I celebrated the day Ameren's Pawnee Call Center offered me a voluntary separation package (VSP). I was more than ready to leave, but still realized this had a spin on it. Companies are very good at coming up with clever ways to make themselves look good even when what they are doing is not. Much as "merger of equals" was in reality a spin of a UE takeover, VSP was a spin on "leave now voluntarily with a little extra money or leave later with nothing". I wasn't really given any choice, but throwing the word voluntary in there made it sound like there was and made it seem less like Ameren cutting personnel whose jobs had been eliminated by the merger.

What did I have to do to prove to God that I'd placed my life in His hands? When would He open the windows of Heaven and pour out a blessing I could not contain? This wasn't how the story went. I was only supposed to have to hold on and trust in God through one trial. Then He in turn was supposed to miraculously provide. Other trials might follow. But the pattern was supposed to be trial, trust, provision, trial, trust, provision. Not trial, trust, trial, trust, trial.

"Where is the provision part of the story, Lord?" I demanded of God. I did not understand why this was happening. Now my job was gone and the best income I'd ever had was gone too.

Maybe that was the problem. When I went from IT to the call center, I really didn't lose anything but position. Would I continue to trust God if I lost income along with position?

In one short year, I walked away from a life raft job that I did not love. Still, I left the call center with my head held high and my sights set on how God would provide for us. Many of my call center co-workers were shocked when I left with such a positive attitude. The company clearly didn't care about me. So why should I care about leaving on good terms? My faith that God had something better for me made no sense to them. They thought I should be bitter and angry. Especially since after fifteen years of dedicated service, this was the **second** job this company had pulled out from under me. First, the data control clerk position under the CIPS name. Now the CSR job under the Ameren name.

For my part, I was positive it would only be a few weeks, or at the longest a few months, before God led me to a job I would enjoy that paid just as well. Instead, God led me into a desert, just as He did Moses, to prepare me to lead others out of their desert. In the desert God changed me from the inside out. Humility replaced pride. Openness to my need for others replaced independence. Creating a career path on my own gave way to acceptance of God's will regardless of where He placed me. God engaged me in the lives of others in ways only He could orchestrate.

Humbled

Opened

Placed

Engaged

*I found **HOPE** in Jesus and Him alone. The process of His transforming work in my life was about to begin.*

My journey toward genuine hope in Jesus Christ began with a step off a cliff. I expected my trust in Him to lead to a better or at least equivalent job. Having the job at the Pawnee Call Center not last long enough to secure another job with Ameren, much less the "luxury liner" position I'd hoped for, was the complete opposite direction of where I trusted God to take me.

The more I did and God didn't, the more my faith dwindled. I played well the role of the good Christian young man during my year at the call center. But God knew my heart was in the wrong place and that my underlying motivation was to not go backwards financially and to recreate the employment success I'd had at CIPS.

Spiritual Application

God leads us a step at a time. God knew I couldn't bear the thought of what was yet to come. His Word is a lamp that lights only a small area ahead of us. As much as we think we need an 800-million candle power searchlight, God knows how much we can handle and when to allow us to see it. Any more, and we would become overwhelmed by knowing too much. Any less, and we would wander aimlessly by knowing too little.

Practical Application

A sense of humor and a positive outlook are essential to have when loss and failure make an unwelcome entrance into your life. Looking back on my year as a customer service representative, I can see much to laugh about. But instead of enjoying the present, I found myself either mourning the past or thinking about how God had to intervene to make my future better. Laughing in the hard times doesn't mean you aren't giving the situation serious enough attention. It is simply a way to make the present better for you and everyone around you. I thought I had a positive outlook, but it was actually more of a presumptive outlook. A presumptive outlook expects things to improve quickly. A positive outlook will stay positive as things slowly unfold for better or worse.

CHAPTER SIX
CHASING THE PAST:
EMPLOYMENT HELL YEARS 2-4

The CIPS "luxury liner" had sailed on without me, the call center life raft hadn't kept me close enough to it to climb back aboard, and my last-gasp hope of ever re-connecting with CIPS was forever relinquished when I signed the VSP. My goal had now become finding an equivalent to my former production control clerk position. While interviewing for a computer production specialist position at the Linq insurance company, I had to know if the jobs were similar in more than just title. To that end, I mentioned jokingly what I had thought was a good description of my CIPS job: "When you don't mess up, no one knows you exist. But when you do, it seems like everyone knows you were the one who messed up."

As soon as the IT manager laughed and agreed, I knew it was the same type of job I'd lost to the merger a year earlier. I accepted the CPS position at Linq Insurance Company, located mere blocks from the CIPS building where I'd once worked. In December of 1998, I was positive I would succeed at Linq. I saw this new position as me starting over not much below where I'd left off at CIPS. I had climbed from part-time janitor to IT in just fourteen years while not living for God. Now that I was living for God, He would surely enable me to climb even higher up Linq's IT stairs in no time. My confidence was once again at its peak. Problem was, that confidence was now more in myself than in God and more a "bring it on world" attitude than confidence in Him.

My new position involved a one-third pay reduction, and I had to go back to the evening shift. Regardless, I continued to tithe. For the first couple years, things looked good. A side job cleaning an office building came along in 2000 to help with the income loss, and about the same time I learned that a special training for programmers was available. I would have to swallow my pride and do janitorial work again as well as eat my words of disdain for the programming profession. But maybe if I accepted whatever jobs God lead me into, God would stop our backward financial slide.

We did end up having the income from the cleaning job for a few years. Unfortunately, when I checked into the programming opportunity, I found that the class that had just finished was the last one they would offer. How much bad timing can one family have in the workplace? My life had taken a serious step backward financially, and I wasn't ready for that. However, success had come easy before, and I assumed it would again.

WRONG! CIPS had a team environment. Not everyone was a team player. But overall, co-workers were more co-operative than competitive. I felt supported there and set up for success. The environment at Linq fell more to the competitive side. I came in with experience this time, but even with experience I had a lot to learn, and I learned it the hard way. The people who were supposed to train me made sure I never knew quite as much as they did. It didn't seem to matter that my mistakes made the department look bad. The more mistakes I made, the better my co-workers looked.

The poor training made the learning curve that much harder for me. Worse, it made relationships with co-workers difficult to keep pleasant. One evening I transposed a three and a four in the computer code that calculated the dividend percentage for Linq stockholders. The next day I found a note that read: "You cost the company $3,000." I'm just glad it wasn't a zero and a nine. The joke after that was, while Linq didn't like me all that much for making that error, the Linq stockholders who benefited financially loved me.

Night shift got old fast. When I heard that someone on the day shift was retiring, I made sure everyone knew I was interested in the position. Unfortunately, it would turn out that with all its negative points, this initial job with Linq was the best one I would ever have there. All later attempts at Linq to generate the same success I'd known at CIPS met with disaster. Goodbye, frying pan. Hello, fire!

It's amazing that jobs you look back on as an awful experience could sound so promising initially. The position I was aiming for—production control analyst—offered daytime hours, a desk of my own, and the opportunity to learn new skills. Ironically, these new skills were to learn something old, even ancient in computer years. It was a mainframe data entry system called Key/Master. All I remember about it now was that it was written in Assembler language, the infancy of computer code from the 1940s.

The company gave me a few months to learn how to write Assembler code. To avoid naming real names, let's designate the person assigned to train me in the Key/Master position before she herself was due to retire by the alias of Meredith. Meredith had held this position for a long time before I came along. As in, she held all the knowledge to herself.

Something about the training felt strange from the start. One unusual aspect of the day shift at Linq was a livestock semi, commonly referred to as the pig truck, that passed each day as day shift ended, leaving a wall of stench for employees to gag on when they headed across the street to the parking lot. Pretty soon I began to wonder if it wasn't a sign that working day shift at Linq would stink as badly as this so-called training.

It might sound mean and was in fact mostly (but not always!) in jest, but if you got on someone's bad side at Linq, they'd say they hoped you'd get run over by the pig truck. Meredith was soon on my pig truck list. All she had me do was read books that required me to already have an understanding of the subject matter. Since I had no training on what I was reading, I learned just enough to be dangerous.

To this point, Meredith had never had a co-worker who could step into her position as a long-term backup. That would require the co-worker to know as much as she did. It became quickly clear to me that Meredith was determined to remain so indispensable the department couldn't survive without her. Which at first made no sense to me since she was planning to retire.

Another co-worker named Linda covered for Meredith when necessary. But even she had only enough knowledge of the position to perform common daily tasks. If anything went wrong, it was back to reliance on Meredith. Meredith told me she would answer any questions I had, but she knew I didn't know enough to ask the right questions. It was the old "I know something you don't know" game, and she was enjoying every minute of it.

After a few weeks of this, I flat-out asked her to let me do the job with her there to guide me through it. She replied, "Read the manuals. That's how they made me learn it. If that's how I had to learn, that's the way you have to learn it too."

It didn't matter that the knowledge she now had was amassed over several decades through hands-on experience. There was no way I could learn Key/Master through the manuals before her retirement date. That was when Meredith suggested Linq make her a consultant. Then if I ran into trouble, she would be available to assist me—for a price.

Now it made more sense why she wasn't teaching me the job. I'm not sure what she had against Linq, but it was obvious she was getting even. I talked to my supervisors about this. They in turn talked to Meredith. But nothing changed. It only got worse, and time was running out. The so-called training I'd received to take over her position made the mediocre training I'd received for that initial night shift position look superb.

In hindsight, I should have refused the position on the grounds that I was not trained properly. In fact, I wasn't trained at all. Instead, I told my supervisors I would learn it on my own and asked them not to expect a lot at first. They liked my determination and told me we would learn together. That settled the panic I felt, but I didn't like the learn-as-you-go method when people were depending on me to do this somewhere close to as well as they'd grown accustomed to with Meredith.

Unfortunately, other than Linda being there to get me through with what little knowledge she had, the "learn together" part never happened. One day she and I had exhausted the few Key/Master resources available and were left with no option but to call Meredith. Meredith knew the answer, but wouldn't help us unless Linq agreed to outrageous terms for her consultation. I had never encountered anything like this in my entire life. It was bad enough that she didn't share her knowledge while she held the position. But what did she have to gain now?

My panic was back. With Linda's help, I muddled through. I was no longer dangerous, but was far from comfortable. At this point the department head, Jason, decided I was ready to take on more. He assured me I would have proper training, resources, time, and support. By now I was tired of a job that made me so uncomfortable and ready to have something I could do well. Doing something well would give me some sort of satisfaction.

The product in question was File Transfer Protocol (FTP). My new job was to handle the transfer of files, mainly to and from the Chicago public school system. For a while, I actually enjoyed this job. I was the contact person outside organizations called to set up secure transfer of information between them and Linq. It seemed to me the worst was now over. There was talk of a replacement for Key/Master, and FTP was off the ground. I was now juggling Linq's oldest and newest computer systems. I had toughed it out, and it was time to reap the benefits of my success.

But it didn't turn out that way. While talk continued, Key/Master was never replaced. I enjoyed FTP, but it was new and I was still in a learning curve. I told myself it was just a matter of time before the glorious day when I could dump Key/Master and master FTP.

Spiritual Application

There is a huge difference between trusting God and presuming on God. I was presuming that God would reassemble my life the way I wanted it reassembled. I was focused on getting some sense of employment and financial stability back. God, in contrast, was focused on teaching me that He is the only source of lasting stability. Once God becomes your stability, the storms of life can rage around you all they want. The storms may shake you up, but with God to hold onto they will never destroy you.

Practical Application

It is impossible to recreate the past, so don't try. Enough said!

CHAPTER SEVEN
DOUBLE TROUBLE

My new job at Linq had started to look like it might work out. I was enjoying my new responsibilities and learning new skills. Then I got sick. I ended up missing so many days of work that I lost all my learning curve momentum. This was the beginning of the end for my time at Linq. The frustration of not being able to get my life back to any semblance of what I could call success was also the beginning of the end of my desire to continue living a life that seemed to keep getting worse by the day.

I was initially told I had a common illness, but what I actually experienced was far from common. I was weak, couldn't keep my fever down, and would wake to a large pool of sweat on my pillow. Several calls and visits were made to the doctor and ER. Each time I was sent home with the same mantra of rest, fluids, and medication. I knew something more was going on. I'd had the flu before, and this was not it.

But what then was it? The doctors had spoken, so I did as I was told and went home to try to ride it out. Then came one day when I felt so weak and tired I didn't think I'd make it from the couch to my bed if I waited any longer. With great effort, I made it to the bedroom, but my bed offered little more comfort. I turned over on my stomach. That was my last voluntary move. My next attempt to shift position made it clear I was in a dire state. I could feel, hear, see, smell, and I wasn't in any more pain than before, but I couldn't move or speak.

My wife and two sons sat in the living room, unaware anything had changed. Panic swept over me as I tried to think of how to get their attention. *I could just wait until Brenda comes to bed,* I thought. *I may have no choice. What is happening to me?*

I hoped for any indication my condition was temporary. After about ten minutes, I could no longer stand my predicament and willed my arm to move. It took all my concentration and effort to move it only a few inches. So began my crawl to the living room. It would have been simpler to intentionally fall off the bed and hope someone heard the thud over the television. But a broken bone was the last thing I needed now, so I eased myself gingerly and far from gracefully from the bed to the floor.

That was the easy part because I had gravity on my side. Moving across the carpet was another story. A snail could have moved faster. I don't how long it took me. I just know it was slow and not so steady. I made it about six feet out of the bedroom when our dog Misti ran over and started licking me. That caused the human family members to notice and rush over to assist me. Though Misti was now getting pushed out of the way, she kept coming back, clearly thinking her kisses would bring me back around. That-a-girl, Misti! As soon as I knew I had my family's attention, I collapsed. That's the way Brenda tells it anyway. My wife and sons tried to help me to a chair, but I was dead weight.

"You're going to have to help us," Brenda urged. With all four of us giving it our all, I made it to the nearest chair. I felt like a life-size ragdoll. Brenda kept her composure and did all she could to figure out what was happening to me. She called my parents. No answer.

Call 911, please call 911, I thought, frustrated that I could not find a way to communicate this. I don't remember much between her calling my parents and my brother-in-law, Brent, showing up. They knew they had to get me to the hospital, but it was cold so they put a coat on me first. I imagine that looked quite comical despite the circumstances.

Now for the big challenge. How would they get me out the door, down three steps, and into the van? Brent bent down and put his arm around my waist. The next seconds were the ride of a lifetime. Flopped over his shoulder, I saw a blur of carpet, steps, ground, and back seat, ending in a close-up of the van floor. My fingers were mere inches from the ground. Had Brent dropped me, my arms would have done nothing to prevent my head from taking the brunt of the fall. I now felt more like a sack of potatoes. I laid half in the seat, half on the floor as Brenda drove me to the hospital. Every few blocks she asked me if I was still with her. I responded "yes" in my head, but don't know if I actually communicated that verbally. I may have made a noise or forced a weak "yeah", but good communication still eluded me.

Once at the hospital, I expected the pace to quicken, but just the opposite ensued. I was left immobile in the van, while Brenda answered questions prompted by her statement that I couldn't move. "What do you mean he can't move? Is he drunk? Is he on drugs?" It was as though the hospital personnel were reluctant to add me to the many people already there. Brenda convinced them my immobility was from neither alcohol nor drugs and persuaded them to come out and get me.

What is taking them so long? I thought as my patience ran out. Once inside, I hoped they would wheel me straight to a room. Instead, I was added to the back of a long line. My mom and dad soon joined us. Standing close beside me, Dad let me prop my head on him so it wouldn't flop all the way forward or back. His closeness helped to calm me.

My long, miserable wait sitting was followed by a long, miserable wait lying down. At least I no longer had to have my arms hanging limp or felt like my head was going to roll off my shoulders at any second. That relief and the more comfortable accommodations allowed me to rest after the initial commotion of questions, IV, and monitor hookup subsided.

Of course with IV comes the need to urinate. Fortunately, I'd come around a little bit, or someone would have had a mess to clean up. This wasn't so fortunate for Brenda, however, since I was still pretty much a rag doll, and she ended up having to hold the urinal. Then the doctor came back in and said they were going to send me home—again!

But this time Brenda was having nothing of it. She convinced the doctor to admit me, explaining that I could barely stand and that she would have to leave me at home alone when she was at work. They finally did admit me. And they admitted she was right also—eventually.

My first night was spent in one side of a double occupancy room, but I honestly believe this was a large single occupancy room that was converted to double occupancy. With my family, including young kids, crowded around me, the clamor was too much for me. I had slipped back into a state of inability to communicate that the commotion was overwhelming me. Nothing personal, but I was thinking, *Get out of here! Everyone please leave!*

I wished I hadn't sent Brenda home. I toggled the whole night between soaking my pillow as well as my entire bedding in sweat and uncontrollably moving my arms and legs in circles. I'm pretty sure the motions weren't a dream, but I couldn't prove it. The next night I had Brenda stay with me, because if it was real I wanted her to get a medical person to witness it. The uncontrolled motions never returned, but other interesting occurrences were yet to come during my hospital stay.

The first such happened when I was being given an EEG (electroencephalogram, which is a test used to detect abnormalities related to electrical activity of the brain). This time Brenda was left waiting and wondering since my routine test turned into a three hour nap. To me the three hours seemed like only a second, so I was puzzled that everyone seemed all worked up over it. The medical personnel eventually determined my "nap" was actually a three-hour seizure brought on by the flashing lights used in the EEG test. To assess me after my "nap", I was raised to a sitting position.

"The room is rolling," I told the EEG tech.

"You mean, spinning?" she replied.

"No, rolling up like an old TV with bad reception," I answered.

Leave it to me to throw them a curveball. That stopped too, and nothing more came of it. But the next day things got really exciting after a nurse checked on me multiple times, then came in to say I was being moved to the intermediate care unit. It seems my heart rate was dropping too quickly, then returning to normal too often for her comfort. My former hospital roommate nearly put my dad over the edge by telling him I was moved to ICU.

By this point, the health insurance benefits I had through Linq had forced me to leave my regular preferred primary care doctor. I was already upset with both my new doctor and the hospital for underrating my condition. Since my condition was clearly far more serious than the doctors or ER personnel had initially thought, despite the continued lack of any formal diagnosis, I expected some sort of apology or explanation. But my primary care doctor acted as if it was all some big joke. He told me my symptoms were unusual for a virus, though he gave no further explanation of why or how it would have traveled to my brain. But evidently *I* was unusual, so that's why it happened to *me*.

What?! He had the nerve to think I would see his shifting the blame to me as funny? This was no joking matter, and I was furious. I requested another doctor to take over my care and promptly changed doctors after my recovery.

No one ever did come up with a conclusive diagnosis, but since there was swelling of my brain, they quasi-diagnosed my condition as an acute inflammation of the brain called encephalitis. The process of getting the mystery virus cleared up and brain swelling down took several more days, and I had more strange sensations like heavy arms, floating, and what was termed as "checking out". I wasn't really all the way out, though. "He's checked out again," I would hear Brenda telling visitors, along with the rest of the conversation. So a note of caution. Just because someone seems like they can't hear you, they still may!

Had my doctor listened to us from the start, my condition would have never deteriorated to the point of affecting my brain. For one, he should have known I was getting worse by the number of calls from us telling him. By the time I was finally taken by van to the hospital, When I was finally admitted to the hospital the virus had already traveled to my brain, and yet he was still telling the hospital to send me home. Through no fault or actions of our own, my family and I were again paying the price for someone else's decision that left a big negative impact on our lives.

Long-lasting effects of encephalitis include a slower decision-making process, difficulty remembering names and other memory issues, difficulty conveying thoughts, and mild myoclonic seizures. While the last could be controlled by medication, the net result of these continuing aftereffects added up to a huge job setback. I was already having trouble getting through the Key/Master learning curve. Now I had missed weeks of work and was having to deal with a brain that processed more slowly as well as memory issues.

In one way, I was glad at the time that this happened, thinking it would force Linq to provide accommodations to ease me back into the learning process that Meredith had made so much harder than necessary, but no such luck. Upon my return to work, I discovered I was expected to jump right back in, despite now having to battle double trouble. All of which served to speed up my downward spiral into despair.

Spiritual Application

Our main purpose on this earth is to bring glory to God. One of the greatest such opportunities that presents itself to us is when we or a loved one are going through a trial. How we conduct ourselves when we are in pain, or when our patience is put to the test waiting for some nurse to return with medication to ease the pain of a loved one, will make us stand out positively from those who lash out unfairly at staff, who are typically doing all they can. When we praise God in times of pain and loss, it gets other people thinking, *There is something genuine here!* Anyone can praise God in times of health, wealth, and happiness. Praising God when He has allowed any or all to be taken from us will make people ask how we can count our trials as "all joy" (James 1:2).

This in turn allows us to point others to the source of our joy, which is our heavenly Father. His love for us is so great that He sent Jesus to conquer sin and death for us. Our relationship with God gives us a joy and peace that "exceeds anything we can understand" (Philippians 4:7). To those who do not have this relationship, the words "joy" and "happiness" may seem interchangeable. But the joy our relationship with God provides is far more than happiness. Happiness depends on what is happening in our lives and around us. The joy that comes from a genuine, personal relationship with God is not dependent on our circumstances. Even when our circumstances are far from anything that would make us happy, we can rest in knowing our loving, heavenly Father is in control and that we can leave the outcome of circumstances beyond our control in the hands of our perfect God. This permits us to rise above our circumstances and experience divine peace and joy even in the hard times.

Practical Application

When visiting someone in the hospital, always put the patient's needs first. Your intentions are good in wanting to be there for them. But too many people around can quickly become overwhelming for a patient. If the patient can't communicate verbally, but can nod or write, it is a good idea to check with them to see if they'd like you to leave so they can rest or simply have less activity happening in the room. A hospital is a hard enough place to avoid unwanted noise and activity without the patient's visitors adding unwittingly to it.

CHAPTER EIGHT
STILL CHASING THE PAST: EMPLOYMENT HELL YEARS 5-6

When I returned to work, expectations for me had increased from learning the basics of FTP to applying it to accomplish the advanced, fledgling task of cross-platform communication. The objective was to use FTP software to transfer information between the mainframe and personal computers (PCs). I knew nothing about PCs and hadn't even mastered the basics of FTP. I appreciated Jason's confidence in me, but the new project itself was far beyond my knowledge. His expectations that I could move the cross-platform project forward while performing Key/Master and basic FTP tasks, especially after the physical toll I had just endured, were totally unrealistic.

Altogether, the cross-platform project was a disaster from day one. All the meetings intended to get the PC team and the mainframe team (a.k.a., me) on the same page ended the same way. A member of the PC team would be assigned to meet with me to explain the PC side of the project. But the different members just kept referring me back and forth between them and giving me vague generalities that were useless in moving the project forward. It was Meredith-style training all over again. A wave of panic swept over me. I knew I was incapable of meeting Jason's ridiculous expectations. Still, what option did I have but to try?

Communication between departments got so bad that upper management called in an outside firm to assess the communication breakdown. The report said the IT department had "silos". It seemed an odd term to use. Having lived in the Midwest my entire life, the first thing that came to mind was a grain silo. What it actually depicted was our inability to share information across separate units of the IT department. I literally begged for outside FTP training and finally got it. I would have to tough it out on my own again, but at least I would get something to work with.

When I attended the FTP training, I presented our cross-platform project to the instructor. That was when I found out it wasn't working because the product was never designed to do what we were trying to do with it. I was given information on the right product and presented the information to my managers. It was turned down because Linq already had too much invested in the current product. I would have to make do with what I had. I needed a backhoe, but was being told to get the job done with a garden trowel. At that point, panic set in full force and never let up for the remainder of my time there.

Shortly after this, Jason called me into his office to update him on the progress of the cross-platform project. I literally had a nervous breakdown right in front of him as I confessed the project was going nowhere, thanks to having the wrong product and no cooperation from the PC team. Nor did I see that changing under current circumstances.

Jason's response was that I was doing fine and to keep working on it. How, as a department head, do you miss that your employee isn't just on the verge of a nervous breakdown, but actually experiencing one in front of your face? On top of that, how do you keep someone on a project after they tell you it's going nowhere and that it isn't going to?

What infuriated me most was that this cross-platform project and other tasks I'd been assigned could indeed have provided the success I was chasing, if only Linq had provided proper training and resources. Instead, here I was, five years into my attempt to chase down and recapture past success, and all I had to show for my efforts was the same pattern of success being briefly within reach, only to crumble into failure in my hands.

✟

I spent many lunch breaks in my car, pulling myself together so I could make it through the afternoon. Even on the days I longed to step in front of the train or the pig truck rather than work there any longer, I found the strength to press on. But the moment I was asked to prepare a presentation to another department on the FTP cross-platform file transfers, which I knew didn't work, I knew I was done.

Though I still wouldn't admit it. I was simply stuck, too panicked to advance or retreat. How could one family have so many out-of-our-control job losses? I mentally recited the list. First, owner embezzlement had cost Brenda her job at Phar-Mor. Then the CIPS/UE merger cost me my job at CIPS. A so-called voluntary separation had forced me out of the Ameren call center life raft into the bitter cold waters of unemployment. All of which had left us starting over three times in just five years.

And now this responsibility for critical tasks with little or no training had me on the edge of starting over a fourth time. Here we were, eighteen years into our marriage with two boys, ages 15 and 12, and instead of moving forward, financially or in my career, I was going backwards. Our entire life felt like a game of *SORRY!* that kept putting us back to the start. Or *Chutes and Ladders* that had us hitting one chute after another. Which wouldn't be so bad if it were just me. But now I was taking my wife and kids down with me as well!

When God had initially provided me with the Computer Production Specialist job at Linq, I had been so sure this was how God would meet our needs. This was the miraculous provision that would make the story end right. If I was content with what I had, then God would take care of our financial situation another way. God would miraculously provide. After all, wasn't that the way the story always ended?

I began to pray as the offering plate passed in front of me, *God, this is money that we cannot afford to give. We trust you, Lord. Provide for our needs as we return to You Your tithe.*

We also tapped every resource available, made sacrifices, and Brenda became very frugal with the food and clothing money. Midway through 2004, I felt my faith start to wane more than it already had. In truth, my "faith" was now more in the miraculous provision story than it actually was in God. I was doing all the right things. So why had God chosen not to bless my trust and sacrifice? What had we done so differently than anyone else that He wasn't providing?

The series of out-of-our-control decisions that had negatively impacted our finances swirled around in my head. Surely we'd experienced more than our fair share of bad breaks. It was time for God to intervene. But He did not. As the resources ran dry and the showers of blessing still did not fall, confusion and frustration chipped away at what little real faith in God I had left.

Where are you, Lord? I cried out. Then, ***Are*** *you, Lord?*

By now I was dying inside, though no one knew this but me. A mental conversation looped over and over in my mind. *I'm a failure. If I make my death look like an accident, Brenda can take the insurance money and start over. She can find someone who can give her the life she deserves. This is no life. This is an existence.*

I didn't eat right and slept little. I should have received a best-actor award for the way I went through the motions. "How are you doing?" someone would ask while we walked down a Linq hallway. I would reply I was doing well, but my next thought would be, ***LIAR!*** I would then hide in the bathroom so no one would see my torment and tears.

During lunch hour, I still went to my car. But instead of listening to Christian radio, I now contemplated ways to kill myself. I often thought of jumping off the fifteen-story Illinois Building in the center of downtown Springfield, the pre-merger home office of CIPS. I wanted to be found at the front entrance with a note thanking upper management for deciding to merge with no thought of the impact they were having on their employees. While I walked to or from my car, the downtown trains, buses, and semis called me to step out in front of them. I wanted to, but I just couldn't.

This went on for months. It began before my bout with encephalitis, but far more so afterward when no accommodations were made for my illness or the time I had missed. Then came the morning of Thursday, November 4th, 2004, when I was finally forced to decide whether to advance or retreat. Advancing would likely lead to a nervous breakdown while I was presenting the FTP cross-platform file transfer. Retreating meant losing another job, which to me equated to financial ruin. Wanting to do neither, I chose to surrender, seeking out what I thought was my only escape—death.

I tremble now at the memory of the spiritual, mental, and emotional death I was experiencing, coupled with my strong desire for physical death. Sundays were especially difficult. Every week the plate passed, and I put in our tithe. But I no longer had any hope that God would bless our faithfulness. And despite the preacher's sermons, I could no longer believe God cared. He had let me die. The final two years of the five years I spent with Linq, I spent as a man without hope.

Spiritual Application

We either trust God, or we don't. It's easy to say we trust God. It's hard to live it out. We are so time-oriented that the longer our trust in God is not rewarded in a tangible way, the more we feel like we are on our own. God is trustworthy. He has promised to never leave us or forsake us. He is still there, even when He allows the storms of life to rage on instead of calming them. In those times, seek Him all the more earnestly. Rest assured that, whether it seems like it to us or not, He is in control. Trust Him unconditionally. He knows us. He cares about us. And He loves us. Nothing He allows us to go through is intended to harm us.

Practical Application

Know when it's time to cut your losses and walk away. I had so many opportunities to admit that I couldn't handle what was expected of me at Linq. When you encounter a no-win situation, the smartest things to do are to retreat and regroup. There is determination to overcome any obstacle to reach a goal, and then there is wisdom in knowing the cost of continuing to move in that direction. Taking the Key/Master position was unknowingly moving from the frying pan to the fire. Staying there was taking a foolhardy *I'm going to succeed at this or die trying* stance.

And I nearly did die trying. There is nothing on this earth worth this. Treat such a situation as you would a literal fire and get out. There is a point where you have to admit the fire is more than you can take on up close. Get out, get help, and get perspective. With help, you can rebuild or move on without what was lost. Facing fire alone to the death doesn't make you a hero or even a martyr. It makes you an independent victim of your own misplaced resolve.

Chapter Nine
Toxic Pride

“**M**ay I help you? Are you OK?”

“I . . . I . . . tried . . . to . . . kill . . . myself . . . today.”

With that, the SIU psychiatry office staff swung swiftly into action. I was immediately taken to one of the small offices. Being a behavioral health center, it was not a typical doctor's office. There was no exam table or medical instruments and supplies, only a desk, two chairs, and a small end table with magazines on it.

The office felt like more like an interrogation room than it had when I'd come in for my earlier bout with anxiety while at CIPS for routine *all is well* appointments. One doctor asked me to provide details of what had just happened. I don't remember much of that brief conversation. However, the events that followed are etched vividly into my memory.

“Is there anyone you would like me to call?”

“Yes, please call my wife.”

"What is her name?"

"Brenda."

I gave the doctor Brenda's number, and she wrote it down. "Stay here. I'll give your wife a call."

The moment the door closed behind the doctor, I fell completely apart. I cried, yelled, and cursed as I hit the back of my head against the wall. A verbal attack on my present employers, prior employers, myself, and yes, even God, followed. Every bad thought and emotion I had kept inside for far too long emerged in one huge explosion of vocal and physical rage. Maybe no one was watching on the camera I could see pointed in my direction up on the wall. But I think someone was. The timing was too perfect for it to be otherwise. I had plenty of time to finish my meltdown before the doctor returned.

"I have Brenda on the phone. She wants to talk to you. Would you like to talk to her?"

"No. I can't."

"Okay, I'll let her know."

I actually did want to talk to Brenda, but the words weren't there. In this state of mind, all I would have done is sobbed. The doctor briefly tried to convince me to talk to my wife, but also recognized I was in no condition for a conversation with someone I loved. As the doctor left again, leaving me alone for a second time, it hit me. How stupid could I possibly be?

"STUPID! STUPID! STUPID!" I berated myself, accentuating each word by banging the back of my head against the wall. How could I ever face Brenda, my mom, dad, or the kids after doing this?

The doctor returned to ask, "Do you think you need to go to the hospital?"

"No!"

"I think you do. There's an ambulance on the way to pick you up."

Great—hospital bills! I snarled mentally. *Just what I need!*

With bills as my first response, I clearly had a long road toward recovery ahead of me. The EMTs endured with professional courtesy my babbling attempts to explain away what had happened. After all, I assured them, I hadn't completely lost my mind. This was only a far overdue release of emotions. And at least I'd taken it out on myself instead of taking revenge on the decision-makers behind the CIPS/UE merger. Maybe the merger hadn't taken my life physically. But it may as well have with the short financial leash it had left me and my family on. There was a big difference between having a life and simply being alive. Not to mention my Linq co-workers, who'd had the opportunity to set me up for success, but chose instead to contribute to my downward spiral into despair.

Once at the hospital, I was asked to sign a consent form willingly admitting myself for psychiatric treatment. You would think I would have realized by now that refusing to sign was not going to permit me to go on my way. But, no. As I continued my futile attempt to explain why I had no need for admission, the dreaded moment arrived. "Your wife and parents are here and really want to talk to you."

"Brenda's mad at me for not talking to her, isn't she?" I responded.

"Yes, she is quite upset, but is more concerned about you than anything else."

I was taken to Brenda and my parents. Everyone hugged and cried. Then the inevitable question was asked. Why?

Of course I had no good answer to why I would do something like this to *them*. My actions suddenly involved someone other than *me*. They always had, of course. Ignoring that fact had just made it easier to justify my desire to permanently end my pain. Not physical pain, though that had been part of it, but emotional pain. The endless search for a way out. A way to make this all stop.

In all of this, asking how I might move forward or who I could go to for support, comfort, and advice had been the furthest thing from my mind. Instead, my *I can handle it!* attitude had surfaced and defeated me. Why didn't I let those who loved and cared about me know how I felt? Why couldn't I explain feeling that I was caught in a no-win situation? Or that I saw our current income as stretched beyond its limits and that leaving my Linq job would lead only to financial disaster?

Each day that I had battled these questions alone had driven me deeper and deeper into depression. Any attempt to explain why I would intentionally inflict so much pain on them was impossible. How much grief would I have caused if I'd actually been successful at my suicide attempt?

Seeing that I was unable to satisfactorily answer why I'd attempted to take my life, our conversation shifted to working our way through individual emotions, pain, and confusion. As the conversation became less strained, I asked, "I look real great, huh?"

"You've looked better," Dad replied.

My family held me accountable for my actions, making it clear that I had a lot of work ahead and hard decisions to make in order to overcome this. They also told me over and over that they loved me and would always be there for me. However, it was totally up to me to either get back up and face my situation head-on or stay down and surrender. I had a support network other patients in the ward could only dream of having. But one Person in that support network, especially, has been with me 24/7. His name is Jesus.

Sure, I faced a lot of external factors that were out of my control. But one factor that I alone controlled could have changed everything. That factor was pride. Pride in my meteoric rise from part-time janitor to a prestigious position in Information Technology. Pride in my home and family. Pride in my success in life in general. Pride in my independence. I had cut off all my support because I was too proud to admit that I couldn't handle my situation on my own.

Did *I* have the strength to get up and fight? Did *I* have the will to start over from the beginning? No. I did not. That would have to come from Jesus. I would also have to swallow my pride and surrender my independence. I would need a network of people, some of whom I was yet to meet. No one can reassemble a shattered life alone.

Spiritual Application

Why is pride so toxic? Pride tells us we can handle anything. That we have it all under control. That we are the masters of our own destiny. In contrast, God tells us that He and only He is in control of all things. He created the universe and everything in it, including us, on purpose and for a purpose. God has a plan, a will, for every man, woman, boy, and girl. But too many of us never live out the life God has planned for us, because that requires surrendering our life plan to Him, and pride keeps us from doing that.

If you are trying to find success as defined by man, let me assure you from personal experience that you are engaged in an exercise of futility. Giving up is typically not the advice given to find success. But in this case, it is the first step that every other step builds on. Give up all attempts to live this life in your own strength and wisdom. Surrender your life fully to God. Accept His Son Jesus Christ as your personal Lord and Savior. Give Him control, and a new life will begin.

Perhaps to others this may not appear to be a very successful life. But I can testify that finding God's will and living it out with God's help and guidance is a far more fulfilling, exciting, and joyful life than anything I could possibly accomplish on my own.

Practical Application

I-trouble is the source of a lot of life's problems. Independence is not a virtue. Ask for help. It benefits you to get another perspective, and it benefits the person helping you to have you need them.

CHAPTER TEN
TOUGH LOVE

What a day! When I'd driven downtown that fateful autumn morning in November, 2004, I certainly had no expectation of spending the night there. My expectations were to either push my increasing desire to die off one more day or go through with my suicide plans. Now here I was, just two blocks from my own workplace, Linq, in the Cygen Medical Center psych ward.

It had certainly been a pointless, roundabout trip. I'd driven to work, done no work, walked to my car to contemplate, driven north to end it all, then back to the SIU psychiatric office to seek help, then endured an ambulance ride under protest to Cygen Medical Center, where I'd been admitted, again under protest, to the psych ward. All that commotion to end up just two blocks from where I'd started! I should have just driven the two blocks to the hospital and skipped all the drama in the middle.

That would have also saved Brenda the drama of wondering why I hadn't returned from work at the usual time, then getting blindsided by a call from the SIU psychiatric office, informing her that I was being admitted to the hospital because I'd tried to kill myself. And to top that off, that I didn't want to talk to her. While it was more that I couldn't speak at that point, it still had to come across to her as my not wanting to.

How Brenda processed all that without verbally taking my head off once she arrived at the hospital is more than I can fathom. Please don't misunderstand. She didn't *oh poor baby* me in any way. She let me know how awful what I had done actually was. Not just this day, but all the time leading up to it. She had no idea how many nights I'd laid next to her with suicidal thoughts without letting her help me deal with them. But she knew this hadn't come about overnight.

"Why?" was the principal question that first night. But a close second was "Now what?"

I didn't want to think about the future. But Brenda knew that if I didn't find a reason to live, I'd just end up relocating from the psych ward to a long-term mental health hospital. Her visits to the hospital were mostly to encourage me. Together we discovered a tiny part of me that wanted help. Was it enough to overcome the part of me that still sought death? No doctor or pill could change the circumstances that brought me here.

Strange as it may sound, I felt more at ease in a psych ward bed, not knowing what tomorrow would bring, than I had in my own bed. In my own bed, I **did** know what tomorrow would bring. That was the problem. I knew tomorrow would bring more of what I already had too much of—stress, frustration, and failure.

Because my attempt to kill myself gave me a high-risk rating, I was initially admitted to that section of the psych ward with "scary" patients who required closer observation. But I didn't find myself the least bit afraid of the other patients. *I* was the patient who most frightened me. I spoke to one of these other patients my first full day there and discovered he was there for the exact same reason as I, right down to the company we both worked for.

Good! I told myself. *Then it's not my imagination that my work environment was a major contributor to my breakdown!*

My time in the psych ward included one-on-one counseling, group therapy, and medication. All this combined with what Brenda and other friends and family did for me helped reduce my stay in the hospital to just one week. But what Brenda did for me after I was released had the greatest impact on our future. I just wanted to take things slow. Imperceptibly slow. Brenda was having none of that. She knew I needed love and patience, which she gave abundantly. But she also knew I needed a reality check and motivation, which she also gave abundantly.

We say today, only half-jokingly, that Brenda kicked my butt back to health. Whenever I would get down on myself and complain about how badly life had kicked my butt and how I would rather stay down than get up and get kicked again, Brenda would respond by kicking my butt for having a defeatist attitude. She would then tell me to get up and trust that God had a plan that involved all areas of my life, including my employment. At the time, that was really hard for me to believe. So Brenda had to believe it for both of us over the next few months and even occasionally after that.

And so the pattern went. Life would kick my butt. Then Brenda would kick my butt and life's butt simultaneously. Then I would get myself back out there to face my fear of life kicking my butt again, not knowing when or if I would ever come out on top again. Along with the lengthy butt-kicking battle royale, God was strengthening and preparing me for something we couldn't see coming in our wildest imagination, using **recovery, clarity, warning signs, support**, and many sources of **love**, as you will see in the following chapters.

Spiritual Application

We tend to retain more of what God is teaching us when we are at the bottom. I was at the bottom, and in my bleakest moments I had no intention of getting back up. But it is in these times that God Himself and others whom He chooses come alongside and lift us up, ignoring our pleas to leave us there because we don't have the strength to move and it hurts too much when anyone else moves us. Once we've reached this point, we have no choice but to admit that we need strength beyond our own. This admission opens the door wide for God to teach us things that we are closed off from when we think our own strength is sufficient.

Practical Application

Allowing a loved one to quarantine themselves from the world out of fear of failure or rejection isn't the most loving thing to do, but the cruelest. Do everything in your power to keep times of isolation to a minimum. The longer a hurting person is allowed to isolate themselves, the more difficult it is to get them to stop hiding from life's realities and face them instead. They begin to feel that being protected from the outside world is something to which they are entitled. Love them enough to tell them what they do not want to hear. Love them enough to motivate them to do what they think they cannot do.

CHAPTER ELEVEN
RECOVERY

"You won't believe me now, but you'll be fine," a nurse told me as I was being admitted to Cygen Medical Center for psychiatric care. "Things won't always seem so bad."

The nurse was right. I didn't believe her. This statement, a relaxation session, and part of a conversation with a doctor are the only interactions with hospital staff I remember. The doctor asked me how I felt. I told him I felt like I was in an airplane that was about to crash. He looked me straight in the eye and told me it had already crashed. I had been referring to my circumstances. He was referring to me. This was no longer about a merger wiping out my dream right after I had achieved it. Nor was it about a sunken life raft or lack of training that set me up for failure. None of that was of any great concern to him. His focus was all on me.

One revelation that came out of my short stay in the psych ward was a single word on a whiteboard: GROW. I had no idea what it referenced, but among the activities listed, it was the only one that grabbed my attention. With little else to do on a psych ward, I figured I might as well satisfy my curiosity by attending an informational meeting about this mysterious word on the whiteboard. That combination of boredom and curiosity would indeed *grow* into something more than I could have imagined.

GROW turned out to be the name of a mental health support group. Despite its capitalization, the name was not an acronym, but simply referenced personal growth. The local GROW fieldworker, Lisa Hensley, was there to introduce patients to this community-based peer-to-peer support program and to encourage them to visit a weekly GROW support group when released. Her love for life and concern for others came through in her genuine smile and words of hope.

What she was promoting mattered less to me than seeing someone so alive who seemed to truly believe there was hope for everyone, even us poor souls labeled a risk to ourselves or others. The words of hope that nurse had spoken on the night of my arrival were unconvincing to me. Lisa's love and concern were believable. I had to find out if she was for real or just really good at getting people interested in GROW's weekly meetings. Other than Brenda and my other visitors, discovering there was free recovery help available to me was the highlight of my time in the psych ward.

The psych ward's treatment program introduced me to the effects of personal decline—depression, addiction, grief, and so on. Through its weekly meetings, the GROW program would introduce me to the causes keeping me from personal growth—lack of meaning, self-gratification, inability to forgive, and countless others. The list of causes was endless, and they each manifested in different ways, but they all led to hopelessness. Or at least a feeling of hopelessness. The GROW program emphasizes that "no one is a no-hoper", and that was an important concept for me at that time.

The criteria to be released from the psych ward were simple. First, I had to answer two questions with a convincing no. Do you want to harm or kill yourself? Do you want to harm or kill others? Second, I had to answer the following question with a hopeful yes. Will you tell a counselor or other trusted adult immediately if you begin to feel otherwise?

I answered these questions convincingly enough to get me released after only a week in the psych ward. But this was far from the end of getting questioned about my mental state. Even after only a short stint on the psych ward, there were required follow-up visits to doctors and counselors, so it was nearly a year before I escaped those three questions. I reached a point where I knew when a doctor or counselor was going to ask them. Near the end of my required visits, I didn't even pay attention to the questions anymore. I just knew to answer no, no, yes. It's a good thing they were always asked in the same order.

But one place I would never encounter those questions was at my weekly GROW meeting. GROW meetings are peer-to-peer, and participants know that all three questions, when asked by medical professionals, amount to the same question. Do you need to be hospitalized? While there was no guarantee, it could be assumed those attending a GROW group were doing so to prevent hospitalization. The GROW program was created to do for mental health sufferers what

Alcoholics Anonymous did for alcoholics or Narcotics Anonymous for addicts. It has its own unique twelve steps and literature based on mental health recovery needs. Unlike AA or NA, GROW meetings are never mandatory, so attendees are more likely to be seeking support of their own free will.

GROW opened my eyes to misery in a whole new light. I'd assumed most attendees would be at the meetings because life had beaten them down. They would be faceless victims of distant people who didn't even know their name. They needed just a glimmer of hope so they could hold on until they caught a break. They would have people who loved them, but didn't know what to do in the face of this sort of situation. They simply required additional support from someone who'd lived through something similar to their situation.

No, that was me. And I was the exception!

The people I met at GROW meetings had never been *up* enough to be beaten down. They were victims of their closest family members. They no longer knew what hope was, if they'd ever known hope. Their family members were embarrassed by them at best. More often than I could have imagined, a family member had disowned them. How sad that the greatest harm was being inflicted by those who were once thought to love them.

My first GROW meeting was all about me. GROW groups are designed to be small, but my first meeting was at a newly formed group that consisted of only the organizer, fieldworker (Lisa), and me. So they were able to spend the time necessary for me to let it all out. Little did I know how good I had it in comparison to the typical GROWer. I later discovered that GROW leaders, organizers, field workers, and recorders are trained to prevent one person from being overly prominent or from "going in circles" with their problems.

But at that first meeting, neither the organizer nor the fieldworker told me how good I had it. Nor did they make any comparison. The only areas of my life in major disarray were all too common employment and financial issues. But to them, loss was loss, pain was pain, and hopelessness was hopelessness, despite their source. Lisa was for real. That night she emphasized two things from the GROW program. First, I had personal value. Second, I was not only a problem person. I was also a solution person. GROW needed me as much as I needed GROW.

For me, though, GROW lacked one vital piece—eternal hope. Searching for a Bible-based support group, I discovered that Celebrate Recovery meetings were held at a church on Springfield's west side, Hope Evangelical Free Church. I loved the large group and testimony time Celebrate Recovery provided. The evening I shared my testimony, a friend from my own church accepted my invitation to attend. He was the person who had missed my "not good, not good at all" cry for help in that tiny church library, so I appreciated his courage and support in showing up.

CR was a refreshing change from GROW, but there was no small group for mental health issues. The closest one was for anger management. If only a group were available that combined the best aspects of GROW with the best aspects of Celebrate Recovery.

That thought was the first time I felt God tug at my heart about sharing what He had brought me through and the hope He had given me. God was asking me to live out II Corinthians 1:4: "He comforts us in all our troubles so that we can comfort others. When they are troubled, we will be able to give them the same comfort God has given us."

I asked Lisa if she thought GROW would allow me to start a special faith-based GROW group. Immediately God began opening doors. First, the GROW leadership gave permission. Then a meeting location was made available in the lower level of WLUJ, a Christian radio station centrally located in Springfield and only three blocks from our GROW group's most dedicated attendee, Debbie Turner. I soon learned that what I'd considered financial ruin was far more affluent than Debbie and her family's ongoing monetary situation. Debbie, along with her husband Harold and daughter Judy, taught me a lot about contentment, living within your means, and the need to swallow your pride when you need financial or any type of assistance.

Through GROW, God allowed me to share the love of Jesus Christ with many people I would have never otherwise met. In my first meeting, I emphasized that Jesus is all-sufficient, but that did not mean Christians were exempt from pain and loss. And that our need for other people to help us get through emotional struggles does not mean in any way that we've lost faith in God.

That first meeting was attended by only two others besides me and Lisa. Sometimes no one else attended. Other times attendance reached into the high teens for so long that

GROW leadership threatened to split it into two groups. A few years later, I felt God tug at my heart once again about sharing the hope He'd given me with a larger audience than this single GROW group. Part of me wanted to stay in the safe confines of this unique group. Another part of me wanted to venture further out into the deep with Jesus. I went through some *but I'm so inept for what you're asking me to do* resistance before finally surrendering to God's call.

I left the group in the capable hands of Debbie Turner, who with her family had become friends of mine. Only an omniscient God could know how the leadership of GROW would change within a few months after my departure. Prayer times and sharing Jesus Christ as Lord were no longer allowed in any GROW groups. Debbie was informed that if she wanted to continue, she would have to do so under the rules of all the other community groups. Debbie asked me what she should do. I advised her that she couldn't truly give anyone hope without Jesus. She stepped down, and the group soon dissolved.

This recovery experience taught me that while the church is a principal place God uses to spread the gospel, it's not the only place He uses. During my recovery, God used a church for a few months and a government-funded organization for a few years. This sounds counterintuitive to how we think God would accomplish His work. But it just proves that God uses whatever and whoever He chooses, even loss and pain, as well as people like me and you who have been impacted by loss and pain.

Spiritual Application

Depression is not a sin. Nor is it a sign that you are not a Christian. Seeking help from a secular support group is no more unwise than seeking out the necessary help for a physical ailment, regardless of whether that help comes from a Christian. Having Christian support in addition to a secular support group is a plus. But the support of others who have reached a point in their recovery that enables them to now help others with their own recovery is an invaluable resource that should not be avoided simply depending on whether or not it is faith-based. Filter advice from any source, Christian included, through the words of Scripture. Placing the Christian label on advice does not always make it wise counsel. Nor does the lack of a Christian label make it necessarily unwise council.

Practical Application

Don't pass up the opportunity to help someone out of fear of what they or others will think of you if you are transparent about your own past. Avoid experience-comparison that either diminishes the other person's pain or makes it seem worse. Avail yourself to them as one who has had a similar experience, and allow them to tell you if they are ready for you to share your experiences with them. Unsolicited advice and *if I can bounce back from my loss, you can too* pep talks are the last things a struggling individual needs.

CHAPTER TWELVE

CLARITY

When someone takes their own life, it leaves their loved ones asking: "What was he thinking?" In truth, every case is different. However, there are some things that all will have in common. By sharing the hopeless thoughts that overtook my mind, I hope to give insight into other similar mindsets as well.

To reveal my mental state immediately prior to and during my suicide attempt, I need to go back first to the initial thoughts that started my downward spiral. At first, they seemed innocuous enough. Everyone has thoughts about how tiresome life is. But my choosing to *outwardly* express so few of my thoughts began a slow, steady buildup of *internalized* irritation with life. Unresolved, my thoughts turned more and more from normal annoyances of life to personalized exasperation.

The intensity of my internal frustration fluctuated, its only outward expression vague hints of futility such as making a circular motion with my finger the moment I awoke each morning. Signifying, of course, silent resignation that today would be another pointless lap that would get me nowhere, so why bother to go through the motions again.

My increasing discouragement came more from within than from the external circumstance. This grew to the point of turning into self-pity. Self-debasing thoughts like *timing is everything and mine sucks* and *I couldn't pick the winner of a one-horse race* increased both in frequency and intensity. It didn't take long for this thought pattern to convince me that I was no longer worthy of enjoyment until I came up with a solution on my own. After all, I had created this mess.

My thoughts were now self-accusing. *How could I have not seen that I was getting in over my head? How dare I think I could climb the Linq stairs and find success that quickly? Why didn't I keep life simple and be content as a courier? If I had, I would still have a job with Ameren. That job still exists.*

Do you see the pattern? It is no longer logical. My emotions have come to the forefront. I am no longer seeing the situation as something life blindsided me with, but as one of my own making. In reality, I hadn't created the situation. It was out of my control all along. But in my mind, I was to blame. Therefore, I was solely responsible to make life right again.

And so the impossible task began. I know now that the solution would have been to relieve the pressure and get help. That in turn would require me to leave Linq. But I'd reached a point where another job failure was more than my pride could take.

I remember one time before we were married when Brenda and I were playing a game of rummy. Brenda won so many hands in a row that it was no longer a game to me. I got mad and threw the cards in her face. I don't expect to always win, but to lose repeatedly without a single win to break it up drags me down faster than anything. I reach a point where to quit is better than to lose again. This is where I was.

I knew at the time I should leave Linq. Pride and fear kept me from doing so. Panic-filled thoughts tormented my mind. *I hate my job situation. If I stay, I will have a nervous breakdown. I hate my financial situation. We are already on the edge of financial disaster due to my previous job losses. If I leave, we'll be living on the streets. Stay and fail. Leave and fail. This is a no-win situation.*

✝

Night after night, day after day, I wrestled with the same question: stay or leave? *I can't stay. But I have to stay because I can't leave. But I have to leave because I can't stay.* Mental and physical exhaustion took hold. My thoughts turned darker and darker. If I left, I couldn't face life at home. If I stayed, I couldn't face life at work. How could I do neither? The only answer was to be nowhere. To simply no longer be.

As I neared the bottom, my thoughts spiraled ever faster. Then I hit bottom. *I'm done. I can't resolve it, and I can't do this anymore. I have to distance myself from this. Now!* That's the day I drove out of town to escape the unsolvable problem that I had created. With each mile that passed, the more comfortable the thought of taking my life became. *If I'm gone from home and I'm gone from work, I may as well be gone, period.*

In a sense, the physical distance actually helped. I had made a decision. I had broken out of the endless loop my mind had been stuck in for so long. Once I found a location, it was only a matter of following through on ending the turmoil permanently. Except that the spur-of-the-moment method I'd selected when my mind snapped at work turned out to be much slower than I'd expected. So now a whole new line of thinking began. My mind jumped rapid-fire from one question to another. But these questions were not circular like the previous ones.

How do I make this an accident or disappearance instead of a suicide? Will life insurance provide for my family? How do I keep the police from finding me or my car? Am I far enough away? Is anyone thinking about where I am? What the hell am I doing?

A breakthrough! Rational thinking was back. Sadly, for many attempting suicide, the method is too quick for the reality of the results of their actions to ever sink in. Suicidal people simply aren't able to cut through the confusion and pain in time. They have hurt so badly for so long that death seems better than living any longer with the pain of rejection, failure, loss, guilt or their physical condition.

Typically, a person contemplating suicide won't mention it to anyone. The decision is too great and too personal. Mentioning it complicates the decision by involving another person. And to what point? After all, if you can't solve your dilemma, someone from the outside certainly can't! Unlike myself, most don't want to leave a mystery. But neither do they want to be deterred from their decision. In their final hours or minutes on this earth, they may try to express all the things they could not say by leaving a suicide note. I have never written or read a suicide note and hope I never do. If I'd tried, I have no idea what I would have written and cannot put myself back into that mindset to the degree that I could write what I might have written then.

Warning Signs

Over recent years, God has given me the opportunity to speak with many hurting people. Through this, I have learned the sign language of mental pain. It is much more subtle than that of physical pain. The person who experiences mental pain is also more likely to go to great lengths to hide it. Fortunately, people sending these messages often do so involuntarily.

To deter a suicide, it is important to learn how to read these subtle non-verbal and nearly unperceivable verbal messages. My wife learned to read these messages after my suicide attempt, and to this day she notices them before I do. Let me share just a few such signs so that you can assist someone to express verbally what they are expressing non-verbally.

Changed breathing: The first sign to surface for me is that my breathing changes. Each breath is shorter and slightly labored, audible, but not quite a sigh. These days that is more of an indicator that I am in deep thought about something. But Brenda is still quick to tell me that I'm breathing funny. I'm not a doctor, but I know from experience this is a sign of stress that is not easily hidden. It may be an involuntary, physical response. I can more easily suppress sighs, heavy exhaling through the mouth, and lip vibration that sounds like a horse. Unusual breathing is a good first indicator that someone is stressed. The greater the stress, the more obvious and continuous the funny breathing is. But there is nothing funny about its source.

Clenched hands: Hands are another sign that is more difficult to hide. If the mind isn't relaxed, the hands show it. For me, they would go into a fist. If my mind relaxed, my hands would relax. The converse was also true. Consciously relaxing my hands helped to relax my mind. For yourself or a loved one, the initial body language may be different. But our bodies don't lie. If something is wrong on the inside, it will show on the outside in some way.

Facial mask: The face also tells a lot about a person's mental state. Most people are good at putting on a mask. Depression isn't something a person likes to advertise. Seeing through the mask requires a deeper, longer look. The eyes will tend to be empty or stare into nothingness. The mouth will be clenched or unable to smile for more than a few seconds. A genuine laugh will also be hard to come by.

You will not find these specific signs on most depression checklists. It isn't that these checklists aren't accurate. They are simply not written from the perspective of someone who is intentional about keeping their mental pain hidden.

Loss of appetite is listed on a depression checklist, and I was certainly experiencing it. But since I was determined to hide any signs of depression that would force me to open up, I ate at home, but didn't eat during work hours. The sign was there, but only I was aware of it. I was never much of a breakfast eater, so during the week I was eating just one meal a day and struggling to do that.

This ties into the opening sentence of chapter one, where I stated that I know what it's like to be dead. The dead don't eat, nor are they hungry. The mind is powerful and can override natural drives for food, enjoyment, intimacy, pretty much anything. When I had to eat to keep from drawing unwanted attention, the mental conflict was incredible. *You're dead,* I would say to myself. *Why are you eating?*

The signs above are pre-cursors to more serious signs, which go beyond staring into nothingness to indicators of a feeling of nothingness. Such serious signs include isolation, not talking, and going through the motions with no signs of life. Alive in body, but not in mind is a place you don't want to let yourself or a loved one get to.

It is natural to want to minimize what you are seeing, and the hurting person will help you do it. So if you are going to err, err on the side of caution. How many times has it been said after a major tragedy that something just didn't seem right, but no one thought it was *that* bad. It may not be, but don't wait too long to make sure.

Spiritual Application

Our thoughts can never become so tangled that God cannot get us thinking straight again. The Bible is so alive and powerful that it can reach deep within us to the thoughts and intents of our hearts (Hebrews 4:12). Once our hopeless thoughts and deadly intents are exposed, God will replace them with thoughts that are hopeful and with intentions to live above whatever crisis we are currently going through. He will accomplish this through His power, which overcame death and Hell. By His power, we will overcome our longing for death to free us from hellish circumstances.

Practical Application

Unless you tell them otherwise, people around you are going to assume you will make it through whatever crisis you are facing. No one can read your mind. If you can't speak it, then write it. Many times the fear of what may happen next if we share our suicidal thoughts is precisely what stops us from taking the first step to break out of that endless loop of hopeless thoughts like *I can't!* and *no matter what I do, it ends badly.*

Conversely, if you see signs in another person that something is wrong, don't ignore them, assuming they will tell you when they are ready. Chances are good they will never reach that point of their own accord. The person in need may also assume that if you are making no effort to intervene, you simply don't care enough to do so.

Also, when questioning someone about their mental state, it is imperative to speak the truth in love. If you are right, your loving attitude will help them open up to you, even if it takes some persistence on your part. If you are wrong, they are less likely to take offense and may come to you if they do find themselves heading in a bad direction mentally.

In my own case, what actually happened when I finally shared my suicidal thoughts was that I received the help I had been in need of for far too long. The help of people who told me "you can!" and that it only ended this badly because I'd waited so long to let someone know of my desperation. Those same people then spoke life back into me with affirming words that assured me my life was far from over. Instead, only one chapter of my life was over. And the closing of that chapter was the beginning of a new one.

Chapter Thirteen
Support

N aming all of the people instrumental in my recovery would be impossible. Lisa Hensley and the GROW organization provided the first spark. Scores more followed, and God knew exactly who to use when. He put some people in my life for mere seconds, while others were already there before I hit bottom and still remain with me for the long haul. I have needed every last one of them.

The people I ran to first were the medical community. I couldn't name the various doctors and counselors I saw on a routine basis. For sure, I couldn't name the receptionist at the SIU School of Medicine's Behavioral Health Office to whom I'd stammered, "I tried to kill myself today." While she was involved for only seconds, I would offer my thanks in person if I knew who she was.

There are so many like her who will never get the recognition they deserve for their small, but crucial role in the restoration of my life. Maybe it's better this way. Every *thank you* would carry the potential to have me bawling like a baby. I no longer need psychiatric care. But during the season when I did, I am thankful they were available to care for me, even when I felt I didn't deserve to be cared for.

The right people for the right season became a theme. There were times I thought God had removed the right people and replaced them with wrong ones. He didn't. His message was clear. *Don't get too dependent on people. I'm the only one you can always depend on.*

Some of the people God used made sense to me. Inside support came from family, friends, and church leaders. Outside support came from support groups and medical professionals. Then there were people who at the time made no sense at all. People whom I thought had nothing to offer gave me a whole new definition of contentment. People who treated me unjustly showed me that I could stand strong. They also showed me I couldn't make everything right in my life, regardless how strong I stood for justice.

Ironically, my initial response to support was often far from positive. Thankfully, I didn't verbalize that response every time. It may be part of the recovery and growth process, but I spent a lot of time upset with those who were most influential in my recovery and growth. I remember Pastor Dave responding to a situation where I had no choice but to walk by faith: "Isn't that great you get to walk on water?"

No! I retorted silently. *It's not great! YOU walk on water, then come tell me how great it is!*

I'm sure now that the pastor's remark was no flippant statement. He could say it because he had indeed walked on water, and he knew from personal experience that if I just kept my eyes on Jesus, then Jesus would make the impossible possible. And if I didn't, Jesus still wouldn't allow me to drown. He would lovingly reach down, pull me up, and remind me to focus on Him while He took care of the threatening waves.

Love Endures All Things

But my greatest support would come from Brenda. When my wife said her wedding vows, she had no idea to what degree they would be tested. I'm pretty sure she wasn't thinking for richer or for bankrupt, in encephalitis and in health, or till suicide do us part—almost. Not once during any of these times did Brenda ever say she regretted marrying me. I wish I were 100% sure I would have done the same.

When I gave up, Brenda refused to. When I felt hopeless, her hope doubled. When I turned away from God, she ran into His arms of love. When I had no motivation, she motivated me. She loved me through everything, but let me assure you that when the situation called for tough love, she was tough as they come.

I have hung in there through Brenda's own hard times, but nothing to the degree of what I put her through. Most couples go through storms together. In our case, she weathered the storm alone, and I was the storm! One thing I expected to hear eventually after my suicide attempt was, "I'm out of here! I can't live like this anymore." But I never heard it.

I have repeatedly asked Brenda to write about her initial response to the news of my suicide attempt and what it was like for her while I was in the hospital. Understandably, she hasn't brought herself to do it. I myself have felt the pain of mentally reliving those events, so I don't blame her for not wanting to think about it. I once presented a short version of my recovery testimony at a GROW function. Afterwards, a man came up to me to ask how I could share such emotional events without breaking down.

My answer was that it had actually taken quite a few times of breaking down during my presentation to reach this point. I hope the man didn't equate that with the cliché that time heals all wounds. In truth, the amount of time that has elapsed doesn't make much difference. What really makes a difference is whether or not you have made peace with the past. I thought I had made peace with the CIPS/UE merger, only to discover along my road to recovery that walking away from the merger with an *I'll show you!* attitude and determination to re-create the success I'd had with them was simply a means to avoid mourning my loss.

Since Brenda has not written down her side of the story, let me do my best to flesh out the ways in which my suicide attempt caused more pain for her than it did for me.

I don't remember Brenda crying much, if at all, during our visits. She did later tell me that she'd called her own mom on the way home to update her on my condition. I'm guessing her mom heard more crying than conversation, since when I later asked Brenda how she had handled my hospital stay, she replied, "I cried all the way home." I'm sure Brenda also had many conversations with our boys, my family, and our church family. Brenda also read the book *Why* by Anne Graham Lotz. The book's theme is why tragedy comes into our lives. How well it helped her answer why I tried to kill myself, only Brenda could say.

Once I returned home, there was a distinct difference in our relationship. Brenda was more aware of how beneficial it was for me to enjoy even the smallest things. Sitting on the front step and letting the sun's warmth relax me was and still is great therapy. Brenda would let me stay out there alone for a while, then come out, rub my back, and say, "Soak it up, sweetheart, soak it up."

Brenda also allowed me to talk it out with a friend who had also attempted to take his life. The topic of those long-winded conversations was mainly an attempt to answer, "Now what?" Brenda was also more protective of my emotions in that she would run interference if the boys started to stress me out. While she eventually weaned me off such emotional protectiveness, the lesson we both learned about the benefits of simple pleasures has stayed with us.

But though Brenda provided me what I needed after such a traumatic experience, some things she would not allow. My bad employment experiences did not give me license to sit around sulking about the past. Or to allow those experiences to paralyze me to the point of being too afraid to look for another job. As I shared earlier, Brenda lays claim to kicking my butt into doing what I had to do, whether I liked it or not.

Rebuilding my wife's trust that I wouldn't attempt to end my own life again took far longer than I expected. Brenda would expect me to call if I was going to arrive home even ten or fifteen minutes later than usual. She would get unnerved if an errand took me longer than she thought it should. For a time, she was even concerned about me go anywhere alone. One day I asked my friend Ed, whom I had driven past on what I thought was my final day of life, how long he thought this would last. Ed reminded me just how long I'd told my wife I was okay when I wasn't and how I'd failed to consider her welfare in my attempt to end a supposed no-win situation.

Eventually, our lives did get back to some sense of normal. But some things will never be the same for either of us. This includes the emotional scars any near-tragedy will leave for the rest of your life. But more significant are the wisdom and strength Brenda and I have gained from taking this journey—together.

Spiritual Application

Fallible as human beings are, God chooses to use us to bear one another's burdens. When we are hurt and let down by others, our tendency is to isolate ourselves. But if we isolate ourselves from every person who hurts us, we will end up isolated from everyone. Though only God can fully bear our burdens, we must be willing to share our burdens with those special people God places in our lives to pick us up when we fall down. We must also allow God to place us in the lives of others, so we are there to pick them up when they fall. Brenda has stayed by my side through far more than most women would, for which I am deeply thankful. That said, only God can truly say that He will never leave us or forsake us. How good it is to rest in that fact.

Practical Application

When it comes to other people, choose wisely what bridges you burn. You never know which one you may need to use in the future. Burning bridges in anger, frustration, and hate often leads to a lot of work rebuilding them or to losing a relationship when rebuilding the bridge proves impossible. The only bridges we should burn are those that lead back to a place of harm for us.

This is especially true of our relationships with our spouses. When we tell our spouse that we love them, there should be no unspoken *because* that follows. We make a commitment to love our spouse, period. Not for their physical attributes, the way they treat us, or the way they make us feel. Many times when Brenda or I have been guilty of an offense against the other, the question of *why do you love me?* has arisen. Sometimes we'll give a silly answer like, "Well, it's a bad habit I just can't seem to break." The true answer is that both of us have made a conscious choice to love the other till death do us part.

CHAPTER FOURTEEN
NOT MY JOB:
EMPLOYMENT HELL YEAR 7

2005 was a year of letting go of my dashed hopes and allowing God to fill me with a new and better hope. Hope in Him. Hope in His plan for my life. It was also a time when I had to apply the many lessons learned in the time leading up to and after my suicide attempt. Though God had given me a second chance at life, another year of employment hell was still ahead of me.

I no longer felt the need to re-create the success I'd had with CIPS. My prayer now was simply for any job that would provide the income and benefits necessary to keep us at our current standard of living. It didn't have to be a job I loved. One I didn't hate would be good enough. At this point, I cared less about the job itself than finding one I could become proficient in. Most of all, I wanted to feel some sense of satisfaction at the end of the day. Too much of my last six years had been spent in disgust of my employment situation.

But after the Linq employment fiasco, it felt awkward to re-enter the workforce. The man who had wanted to take on any challenge now wanted to ease back into a job. Despite my recovery, my ego and confidence remained low. I had a proper perspective of myself as God's unique creation. I knew I was placed on this earth on purpose *for* a purpose. But as an employee, I didn't feel up to any challenges yet.

Some might see my abandonment of an IT career or even the electronics field I'd studied in college as giving up on myself. In reality, my decision was based more on no longer feeling any need to seek out a high-paying career. When I came across a supply clerk position, it seemed a fresh start away from the high pressure of working in IT.

My greatest concern was being told I was over-qualified, so I preempted that by informing Human Resources that I was starting over after a bout with mental health issues. Though I didn't go into details, I would later regret revealing more of my past than necessary. The orientation session emphasized no form of harassment would be tolerated. If such occurred, employees were encouraged to go up the chain of command as far as necessary to rectify the situation. This all sounded wonderful.

Other than being back on a nights and weekends shift, I enjoyed my new job. The supply clerk position consisted of six main responsibilities: order, receive, deliver, stock, fill, and clean. Each clerk was assigned one of these tasks each day, but assisted with the others as necessary. If I'd been single, I might well have stayed on the night shift since the pace was much slower than the other two shifts and paid better. But the work schedule was inconvenient for normal family life.

Even so, coworkers warned me I was better off staying on the night shift. By now I'd heard day shift horror stories. I'd even noted that the handoff from night shift to day shift could be confrontational. The day shift coordinator, a woman I'll give the pseudonym of Kate, seemed to be always in a bad mood. Her mistreatment of others and attitude that she was somehow the boss of our department, Central Supply, made a good shift turnover nearly impossible.

Our actual supervisor, a woman I'll call Erin, fed into Kate's abuse of authority by allowing her to confront and reprimand other department employees, especially male employees. Still, I paid little attention to tales about outright harassment and discrimination of males on dayshift. After all, this was a company with zero tolerance for harassment.

How naïve I was!

Despite the warnings, I applied for the day shift position. This was just some power struggle, I assured myself. If I did good work and let Kate think she was in charge, we'd get along fine. After all, if our supervisor, Erin, could let Kate think she had more authority than she really did, so could I. And in the beginning, this seemed to work. One day while she showed me the computer system, which was simple compared to what I'd worked with before, she told me I was a keeper.

Yes, Kate and I can work together! I thought joyfully.

In contrast, I noticed one male clerk who could never meet Kate's expectations. While I simply refused to get into it with her, he would defend his actions, resulting in arguments several times a day. Soon he could no longer take Kate's constant accusations about his job performance and found another position.

That was when I discovered he'd been my buffer. The department had only one other male employee, Mike, and he'd found his safe haven in the equipment decontamination room. That he chose to stay in there to avoid Kate spoke volumes. The "decontam" job involved collecting, cleaning, tagging, bagging, and restocking medical equipment that could be re-used. The most common items were IV machines, a variety of pumps, large trash cans, and commode frames. To decontaminate all this safely meant a lot of time gowned up head to toe, including a face shield, a hot, sweaty, nasty job.

With one male gone and the other tucked away in "decontam", I became Kate's sole remaining target. While I'd witnessed her confrontations with other males, I'd chosen to start Kate off with a clean slate when I moved to the day shift. Surely the other guys had done something that set her off. If I could discover what it was, I could figure out how to avoid Kate's wrath.

But the slate didn't stay clean for long. It turned out that being male was all it took to make it onto her list of people to harass. All day every day, I was enduring a constant, just-enough-under-the-radar attack. While the attack was spearheaded by Kate, our supervisor Erin turned a blind eye to it. Most of the harassment came in the form of verbal abuse. Most of the time Kate didn't curse or yell. It was more subtle, such as setting up "Catch-22" no-win situations.

The no-win situation I remember best was product location. If I took too long in her opinion to find a product, Kate would explode, "If you can't find it, you need to ask me!" But if I did ask her, she would snort with exasperation, "You should know where it is!"

In contrast, a female clerk could take longer to find a product or ask Kate for the location and receive a cordial response. There was one female clerk who refused to play Kate's game, and she received the same treatment the males did. I was intelligent enough to know one big happy work family was unattainable. But after all I'd been through in the workplace, this injustice was unbearable. There had to be a way to find common ground. If an affable work environment wasn't possible, professional would have to suffice. One day Kate noticed my frustration with her.

"What do you want from me?" she barked.

Taken off guard, I fired back, "Professionalism!"

A brief debate on unprofessional vs. professional conduct concluded with Kate sniping "Professionalism? I get my work done."

That how she treated her co-workers was part of professionalism clearly eluded her. I had no reply to such obvious blindness. Other males, such as my buffer before he left, had found their own ways of dealing with Kate. I figured I'd nothing to lose, so decided to expose the situation. I knew an isolated incident reported by one person wouldn't be enough. I asked Mike to back up my claim that when a female went on break or lunch, Kate would make sure work didn't backlog, but didn't afford males the same courtesy. If that wasn't bad enough, she would then use the backlog she'd caused as evidence to make the males look bad to our supervisor, Erin.

I also began keeping a detailed journal of each incident of harassment, including time and place. One such entry involved answering the phone for Kate when she was absent and taking a message for her on the nearest Post-it® pad.

Instead of a thank you, I was dumbfounded when Kate yelled at me, "Don't use my Post-it® notes! Get your own."

Since my supply deliveries took me around a huge building, I carried a hand radio, which was kept turned on at all times while on that assignment. But in much of the building, reception was poor. I had just managed to combine two deliveries to the same location into one, which took longer than my originally scheduled trip, but much less time than making two trips. Surely a win, win, win for Central Supply. But not to Kate, who met me in the hallway, yelling at me for being out of contact so long.

"Why don't you have your radio?" she shouted so anyone along that hallway could hear. I popped my radio off my belt to show her. She sneered, "Helps if you have it turned on!"

"It is on," I replied mildly.

"So why didn't you answer me? Why were you gone so long? Where were you? You can't have taken that long to make one delivery!" she ranted without ever giving me a chance to explain.

Despite all this and countless other such incidents, I made numerous attempts throughout the year to make peace with Kate. On one early attempt to apologize for having responded using Kate's same ugly attitude and tone of voice, she smugly replied, "Is that all you've got?" Later, when I actually begged for a truce, she only laughed evilly, but her facial expression and body language said it all. *No truce. I got you to back off. I'm not backing off. I win.*

If I tried to defend myself in any way to Erin, she would always take Kate's word as gospel truth. To me, it seemed that Erin had abdicated her own role to Kate. I spoke to the department manager and Human Resources at length to no avail. As those avenues came to a dead-end, I found myself setting up a meeting with a vice-president.

I'm not sure how word got back to Erin, but it did. Before I could meet with the vice-president, she called me into a meeting of her own. In hindsight, I should never have let it go as far as it did without asking for a mediator. The entire meeting turned out to be nothing more than Erin badgering me to admit that my poor job performance was at fault, not Kate's actions. It didn't matter that Erin herself had just given me a good performance evaluation for the year, or that I'd received two notes of appreciation for improvement suggestions that were implemented. Even when I demonstrated that Kate's accusations were unfounded, Erin continued to defend her. Again and again, she insisted that our meeting was to discuss the problem, not to discuss Kate.

By this point, the days of increased badgering had gotten the better of me. I had already popped out of my seat in anger a couple times. At last I could hold in no longer the four words that had been on the tip of my tongue for most of the meeting. Bolting out of my seat, I slammed my hands on Erin's desk and shouted in her face, "KATE *IS* THE PROBLEM!"

I then exited her office, intentionally slamming the door as hard as I could. I took two huge strides, then spun around. Opening the door again, I stuck my head back inside to announce, "I'm going to the president, and I'm getting a lawyer."

I then slammed the door as hard as I could a second time. To this day, people have trouble reconciling my calm demeanor with this event. Everyone has their breaking point, though, and Erin had found mine. I did exactly as I'd told her and headed straight for the presidential floor. I'd been there just days before to set up my meeting with the vice-president, and it was the only safe haven I could think of. Every part of me wanted to run, but I held myself back to a determined, fast-paced walk. I arrived out of breath and in tears.

The secretary who'd set up my meeting had seemed sympathetic to my situation, so I explained to her that I'd feared something like this would happen. I was sure this was my chance to take the president up on his open door to report harassment. After all, I'd taken all the proper steps. I had gone up the ladder one rung at a time. But now it was time to skip the vice-president rung and go straight to the man who had assured my group of new hires there would be zero tolerance for harassment.

It took me a long time for me to compose myself. I had never snapped like that before and was now beginning to regret my actions. I realized I'd given Erin exactly what she wanted. I would have to explain that I'd been driven over the edge. Proper supervisory protocol would have been to table the meeting the first time I popped up in anger. The biggest hurdle was that it was my word against Erin's as to how the meeting was conducted. The only thing I had going for me was that I had reported the harassment to many people over a period of several months and told them that a confrontation of this sort was not only possible, but likely to happen. That had to carry some weight.

I was brought into a room where I expected to speak to a representative of the president, if not the president himself. I was taken aback when instead I saw security officers and a host of others. What had happened to the sympathetic understanding I'd received here days before? Or to their policy of wanting harassment to be reported, even if it meant taking it all the way to the top?

I knew then that Erin had called ahead to report a skewed version of our exchange that made me look insubordinate and her appear in the right. She had very likely also played the "crazy" card I'd given her at the start when I told her I was starting over after battling with some mental health. I was so stunned that all I could do was start laughing. Which of course made me look all the more mentally unstable.

I had my say, but knew it was all over. To add insult to injustice, security escorted me to the emergency room for a psychiatric evaluation. I did get a bit of validation from the doctor who conducted the evaluation. She understood human behavior enough to believe that what I told her had really happened. If this did me no good with my employer, at least she reported that my outburst was a normal human response to what I had experienced.

The next day, I received a call at home to inform me that I'd been terminated. I'd failed to reach my company's president, but I did get a lawyer and filed a sexual discrimination lawsuit. Once enough time elapsed that I was calm, I went to the Human Resources Department to get a copy of my files. With these in hand, I could start the legal process. But when I made my request, I was asked to wait. About the time I began to wonder what was taking so long, security showed up, and I was escorted out for a second time. I could understand getting security involved when I lost my temper and stormed to the executive floor. But was I that much of a threat just asking for my file?

The lawsuit entailed just one hearing. The employment bureau had already reviewed my good performance evaluation and all the specific incidents I had chronicled in my journal. But their legal counsel advised me to drop the case. She said I had enough evidence to win if the case was against the specific department where I'd worked. However, the way the law was written, I would have to prove the entire company was guilty of sexual discrimination. For my part, I was eager to drag this injustice into the public eye, even if I knew I couldn't win. But with great reluctance, I took their advice, dropping the case to focus instead on recovery from yet more loss and injustice.

It is at this point where too many people make the tragic decision to take matters into their own hands. All legal steps to right the wrongs done to them have failed. Unable to allow the guilty to walk away unpunished, they resort to vigilante justice. For me, this line of thought went no further than telling a few friends that if I'd known how it would end, I'd have given my boss a legitimate reason to call security. Which is another good reason God doesn't let us know in advance how things will play out!

During my recovery from the depression and despair that led to my suicide attempt, God had shown me that it was not my job to right this wrong at the hospital. Instead, God wanted me to pray for and bless those involved. It took me a long time to get to that point. But today I can say in all honesty that I want the best for all involved in this final employment hell. I pray most for the two who headed up the discrimination. I would much rather see them accept Christ's love and forgiveness than have to give an account to God on judgment day.

Seven years, three jobs, zero success. That's what it took to bring me to the place I should have been all along—on my knees with no stipulations. I was broken, lost, and needing God to show me what to do. Kneeling beside my bed, I buried my face in the comforter and wept before Him. As I wept, I prayed:

Dear God, make it clear where You want me employed. I no longer care what it is, where it is, or what it pays. Please show me clearly. I want to know without a doubt that You are placing me where you want me. I am so sorry for not giving You total control until after I have no where else to turn. Lord, do not allow me to take control back. I have made such a mess of my life. Please forgive me for putting stipulations on my prior prayers. I am so lost. I am so afraid. I don't know what to do. Please help me!

I don't know how long I prayed, but it was not short. God must have been ready to tell me to get up and stop blubbering. Regardless, He heard me and led me to a job I would have never chosen for myself.

Spiritual Application

God can't lead a stiff-necked individual. Unwillingness to drop our own desires and submit to God's plan for us only leads to God giving us our way. A way He knows isn't going to end well until we get over thinking it is our job to change what only God can change and begin entrusting our lives into His control.

Practical Application

Not everyone has to know everything. I thought I was being upfront and honest when I let my supervisor know this my first job after suffering a mental breakdown. To her, this was only ammunition to use against me.

Also, there is often more than one right way to complete a task. So be cautious about demanding why your spouse, child, or co-worker is doing something a certain way without first determining if how they are doing it is actually wrong or simply different. By the end of this particular employment, I was sick of being asked why I was doing something a certain way. The question wasn't really whether or not I was doing it wrong, but why I wasn't doing it the way my immediate superior would do it. Admittedly, there are good, better, and best ways of doing things. And sometimes there are required ways to do things, whether they make sense or not.

But even if the job is being done wrong, or not according to specification, *why* is not the best word to start with, though you may want get to that later, because that initial *why* automatically puts the other person on the defensive. Presenting an alternative method, or explaining instead of asking why a task needs done differently, will make a lot of difference in the resultant response.

CHAPTER FIFTEEN
THE TRAGEDY THAT WASN'T

Injustice is hard to take. When we are wronged, our first instinct is to make it right. As children, we've all exclaimed, "That's not fair!" No one has to teach us to defend ourselves. When we are mistreated, defending ourselves comes naturally.

Nor does it take long to find out that much in life really *is* unfair. In fact, it could be argued that everything is unfair. It just comes down to whose favor it is unfair *in*. Unfair is okay until we are the ones treated wrong. We even take for granted those things that are unfair in our favor, such as the creature comforts the United States enjoys, which many people around the world live without. With this entitled attitude, it doesn't seem at all out of line for us to get bent out of shape when we don't get something we think we deserve. Combine this with our desire to keep on par with our peers, and we've set ourselves up for a lot of pity-parties.

There are, however, times of true injustice. These are the large-scale wrongs we feel we must avenge. We're determined to come out on top. There is no statute of limitations. 9/11 is a good example of this. One hotel sign in Springfield still proclaims: "Remember 9/11. Never ever forget!"

Then we have our personal 9/11s. Divorce. Foreclosure. Bankruptcy. Wrongful termination. Major illness. Most of us have a major event in our life we'd honestly like to forget, but which is seared so deeply into our mind it cannot be erased from our memory. Of the personal 9/11s I just listed, I have experienced the last three. During each, I wanted to take matters into my own hands and/or stay tucked away in the pit of despair, where it was safe and people handled me with kid gloves, instead of climbing out to face life's challenges.

During my first couple days on the psych ward, becoming a permanent resident of a safe place free of responsibility was actually appealing. But vacation from the real world came at the price of enduring days structured by other people. Of personal stigma. Of no freedom to go anywhere, which was the worst of all for a person like me who loves seeing new places.

Beyond all that, the desire to wreak havoc on the people and places I saw as the source of my tragic situation was never far from my mind. When I saw Ameren's *All Is Right Again* advertisement on a ground floor window, I felt like shattering it with a rock inscribed *Not For Us Whose Jobs You Took!* When my supervisor set me up to get fired, I felt like choking the life out of her. And I could hardly forget the tragedy that almost was if I had just chosen a quicker, surer method of taking my own life.

If I'd carried out my fantasized responses to the injustices life brought my way, it would probably have resulted in commitment to a mental institution, imprisonment, or death. The only reason none of these were my fate is because God intervened, directing me away from insanity, revenge, and suicide whenever I turned in those directions.

Stories of workplace, school, and domestic atrocities garner newspaper headlines and major television coverage. I do not condone the actions of people who commit these heinous acts. But there is always more to the story than their furious rampage. They didn't wake up that morning and decide to go on a killing spree. Real or imagined, there was typically a terrible injustice they chose to avenge through bloodshed.

Let's take a look at the factors that could have led to my own headline-worthy tragedy. I have a mental illness history, multiple job losses that had nothing to do with my performance, financial instability, discrimination, and harassment. After being pushed over the edge by my supervisor for attempting to address a hostile work environment, I am wrongfully terminated, according to the psychiatric evaluation, for having a natural reaction to the situation. A single one of these has been enough to make people go on a violent rampage.

When all legal avenues are exhausted, some people do decide to take matters into their own hands. Without having God to fall back on as the ultimate Judge who will make all things just in the end, they attempt to get their justice now. As result, the non-headline-making injustice turns into a headline-making tragedy.

In truth, how many people do have a similar story? How many people all across our country and around the world live the rest of their lives with the negative impact of an injustice? The people who should make headlines are those who respond to injustice *without* violence. When mass layoffs happen, an article should be written praising the laid-off employees for persevering. Compare the number of people whose lives have been turned upside-down by an executive decision to merge, downsize, or close their place of employment to those who have actually retaliated violently in any way.

We shouldn't be surprised that violent retaliation happens, but rather that it doesn't happen more often. For too many corporate conglomerates, employees are less human beings than they are human resources. Synonyms for *resources* are possessions and property, which is how too many employees feel treated. But only a tiny fraction ever meet such injustices with violence.

Will I ever forget the injustices I've experienced?

No.

Will I erect a sign in my brain as a daily reminder to keep my personal 9/11 alive with all its emotion and desire for retribution?

No.

In order for me to move forward, the sign had to come down. It is difficult even now to write about it. For many who have suffered similarly, it is still an open wound. None of my words or empathy can heal them. I can only point them to the One who has the power to heal that deep of a wound— Jesus.

Spiritual Application

Jesus, in the well-known passage called the Lord's Prayer (Matthew 6:9-15), teaches us to pray to God, "Forgive us our trespasses [sins/debts] as we forgive those who trespass against us (v. 12)." This makes clear that we are to forgive others as generously as God forgives us (vv. 14-15). We have trespassed, or sinned, far more against God than anyone will trespass against us. Forgive the injustice, and return good for evil. You may never have the opportunity to forgive those who've been unjust to you face to face. But you must have forgiveness available to them, should they ask for it.

Practical Application

Forgiving does not mean forgetting. However, you should use the past only to learn from it. Do not remember and fantasize about getting even. Do not remember to belittle those who were unjust to you by retelling their actions against you to others again and again. If sharing what was done to you does not come from a heart of love for everyone involved and a purpose of helping the one you're telling, then it is best to keep it to yourself.

CHAPTER SIXTEEN
HOPE AT LAST

I had prayed from the start that God would lead me to the right job. However, it took three job failures for me to come to the end of myself. At first, my prayers were for God to recreate the past and make it even better than it was before. I expected immediate action on His part. I wanted a miracle. I prayed that it was for His glory, but I know now that it was actually more for my comfort and security.

When that failed, I lowered my expectations of God and was ready to start again from the bottom. My goal remained eventual success in the information technology field. It took six years to reach the conclusion that past success was gone and would not be recreated either by a miracle or by climbing up from the bottom. At this point all I wanted God to provide me was an employer with training, resources, and a good work environment. Instead, I ended up in the worst work environment of my life. So now what? When would my employment nightmare end? Where did I belong?

I didn't realize it at the time, but the reason my prayers hadn't been answered the way I wanted was because I had stipulations on all of them. After seven years of asking God to give me my way, I finally asked Him to show me clearly where He wanted me employed. No stipulations. I didn't care what, where, when, how much a job paid. I just wanted whatever He wanted for me.

After full surrender to God's will, you might think God would finally put the happy ending on my story and bless me with my dream job. But, no. God made me follow through on my promise to follow wherever He led. The position God led me to was that of a habilitation specialist at the Hope Institute for Children and Families, a residential school for children from ages 5-21 with developmental disabilities, mainly autism. My job as a habilitation specialist was to assist these children with daily tasks.

This may sound like a job that left me with a sense of accomplishment and satisfaction at the end of each work day. It did. It also left me spent. In my short time as a habilitation and education specialist, I was punched in the stomach, slammed against a wall, and knocked on my backside. The latter, to my chagrin, by a girl. I also had feces thrown at me.

While I could have done without these experiences, I loved the job. I didn't just work for Hope. I worked for the kids who resided and attended school there. They inspired me with their dogged determination to enjoy life in the face of so many challenges. I strove to do all I could to improve their lives. I had gone from controlling critical data to changing the diaper of an eighteen-year-old. But I was where I belonged. I was where God wanted me. I was content as 2006 came to an end. 2007 could only get better.

As much as I loved it, the habilitation specialist position was so physical that I couldn't see myself doing it until I retired. Still, I was ready to stay as long as that was where God wanted me. That was when God gave me the job I have now, which is the best of both worlds. As the data-processing specialist for Hope's Behavior Department, I work with computer applications, but no longer have the pressures of an information technology environment. I create and maintain Excel spreadsheets that behavior specialists use to track trends and address them through behavior interventions and medication. I also schedule the kids for clinic appointments where the behavior specialists discuss the kid's progress with a psychiatrist.

I know God has a sense of humor, along with knowing who and what we need to mature us. I prayed for hope, and God gave me both a support group at a church named Hope and a career at Hope Institute. The greatest hope He gave me is the hope He offers freely to everyone. The eternal hope of life after life with Him in Heaven.

Spiritual Application

Many times we don't go where God wants us to go because we can't see that the initial uncomfortable, frightening place He leads us is the only path that leads to doing what He has created us for. Not only was this the case for me when I began working at the Hope Institute, but also when I began the process of writing this book. All I wanted was to sit down with an author, tell them my story, answer their questions, and have them do the writing. I kept trying to hand this book project off. I told God and others many times that He had chosen the most inept person for such a job. But God just kept reminding me that He intentionally picks the most inept person for the job, so that He alone gets the glory.

Practical Application

Coming to the Hope Institute after holding far better-paying and more prestigious positions took a lot of pride-swallowing. But what Hope may lack in pay and prestige, they more than make up for in job satisfaction and work environment. Leaving at the end of the workday with my sanity intact is reason enough to call it a good tradeoff. No job is worth sacrificing your mental health.

CHAPTER SEVENTEEN
FILING CHAPTER-7

When I began working at the Hope Institute in November, 2006, I had finally surrendered my will to God in the area of employment. Unfortunately, the damage of chasing after an impressive job title and corresponding income had already been done. I'd toggled back and forth so many times regarding if and why I was tithing. I'd tithed as a means to a greater monetary return from God. I'd tithed when I had it so God would continue to bless. I'd tithed in thanks to God for providing me with the job at the Hope Institute.

Problem was, I'd never tithed with my heart and mind focused solely on cheerful obedient giving out a heart of love for all Christ had given me that I could never repay. There was always that ulterior motive that God would tangibly bless me for my financial sacrifice. So when that didn't happen, I would stop, always justifying that God understood I could not continue to give what I didn't have. God was supposed to have provided the financial means for me to continue to support His work. I'd heard it said so many times and so many ways, such as:

God has a bigger shovel than we do; when we shovel our little to Him, He will shovel His much back to us.

God will make you wiser with your money when you tithe. You will go farther on nine cents out of a dime with God than you will on the whole dime without Him.

God can take a budget with a tithe that doesn't work on paper and make it work by providing more income or preventing/eliminating expenses.

I heard this mostly from the pulpit. But church members would also praise God for doing these very things in their own lives. Was it because my heart and mind weren't right that it never turned out that way for me? Or was it just cleverly veiled prosperity theology that I was being taught?

I began tithing when God provided me the initial job at Hope. By then I thought I had this all sorted out and was confident I would not stop tithing. I would cut my budget anywhere I had to in order to continue to tithe. Brenda was in agreement, even to the idea of consulting a financial counseling service. This was not the first time we'd visited this same service. We'd sought advice after our liquid assets began drying up and our consumer debt began maxing out. The counselor had asked if creditors were calling us at all hours.

"Not yet," we responded.

"Then continue what you're doing, and you'll be fine," he assured us confidently.

We'd walked out then with a false sense of relief that our situation wasn't as awful as we'd thought. This time we knew we needed help, especially if the tithe was a non-negotiable. We walked in to the financial counselor, knowing this time we really needed assistance. But we were in no way prepared for what we were told.

"You're past the point where our program can help you," the counselor said just as confidently as the former counselor had told us we weren't yet to the point where this type of help was needed. When we told her what we'd been advised on our last visit, she asked who we'd spoken to then. All we could remember was that we'd spoken to a man.

"We could and should have helped you then," she said. "Now it's too late. Your only option is to file chapter-7 bankruptcy."

At her advice, we stopped paying our creditors and told them we were filing for bankruptcy. What a humiliating time this was! Only a couple years had passed since God showed me the way out of employment hell, and now I was entering a bankruptcy hell. *I tithed myself right into bankruptcy,* I thought over and over. I said it out loud many times as well. Though I don't think I ever had the nerve to say it to anyone but myself.

If anyone suggests that bankruptcy is the easy way out, don't believe them. I've never had my taxes audited, but I can't imagine that it is any worse than filing bankruptcy. And to add insult to poverty, you have to pay a lawyer up front to prove to your creditors that you can't pay them. Without help from Les and Dodie Morgan, a wonderful Christian couple, we would have had to delay filing until we could rob our creditors long enough to pay for a lawyer. Every financial detail is scrutinized. It's not good enough to admit you are in financial despair; you have to prove it.

I was okay telling everything except that we gave ten percent of our gross income to a church. I was concerned our church might get pulled into this mess, and I didn't want that. In brutal honesty, I also did not want that fact to prevent me from being able to file. Once again, our tithing came to a screeching halt. Even with the tithe factored out of our financial situation, we had more than sufficient proof to file. We gathered up the required documentation and presented it on May 19th, 2008, along with a check for $674 to our lawyer so he could create more documentation for our creditors and us.

This cycle repeated itself until August 11th, 2008, when our financial failure was finalized in, of all places, the Illinois Building where I had enjoyed my early career/financial success until the word "merger" ended it. To add even more humiliation, we were required to go through credit counseling, which if we'd received when we first sought it out may have prevented all this. Somewhere between May and August, 2018, we will put bankruptcy behind us. It's not the easy way out, but we were told it was our only way.

Spiritual Application

We can never place God in our debt. As the Gospel hymn says, "Jesus paid it all; all to Him **I owe**." God owes me nothing. If I could live a million lifetimes and spend them all in service to Jesus, the ledger would still read all to Him I owe and God owes me nothing. The reason for our bankruptcy was not that we were tithing. It was my attitude that God had to make the ends meet if I tithed.

We must obey God without crossing the line from trusting in Him to presuming on Him. If obedience to God leads to results we don't like, we must still continue to trust and obey. God rarely immediately rescues us from the consequences of our past poor choices. He instead gives us the wisdom to make changes if the results of our actions can be changed, sometimes over a long period of time (in our case, bankruptcy resulting in ten years of fair credit at best!). If the resulting circumstances are irreversible, such as when King David had Uriah killed in order to take his wife, Bathsheba (2 Samuel 11-12), God's mercies are new every day, allowing us to live for Him in the present, no matter how bad our past.

Practical Application

Bankruptcy is not a quick fix. Ensure that all other options are exhausted before even considering it. In hindsight, I'm not sure if I would file bankruptcy if I had that choice to make again. An expert in these matters was telling us it was our only option and that the creditors know the risks of lending. Should I have made greater sacrifices to pay my creditors despite the job losses and medical expenses that contributed majorly to our financial collapse? My only answer is that I don't know. This I do know. If I could do it over again, I would have spent more time in prayer and taken more time to make such a major decision.

CHAPTER EIGHTEEN
SMALL DIFFERENCES, BIG DIFFERENCE

According to a song by American country music singer Wynonna Judd, a little bit of love goes a long, long way. There are many other things that require only a little bit of that make a big difference.

Thirteen years after my despair and initial suicide attempt in 2004, my life is not markedly different. The big differences are that I have a different job and my kids are now grown. Jordan is married, while Shaun is home from college, transitioning to life independent of his parents. But neither of these big differences are the reasons I enjoy my day-to-day life so much more. On the contrary, it is an ever-growing list of small pleasures I did not have before or could no longer enjoy due to my focus on the major calamity that today make all the difference.

My original main problem area was the workplace. Have there been any huge changes? No. The change that stands out most is that my current colleagues work in cooperation with each other, instead of in competition. I'm sure that was true in many departments of the companies I worked for previously, but not in my own department.

My current co-workers appreciate our cooperative work environment, but not as much as I do, since they haven't experienced a prior unbearable work environment for comparison. I've expressed my appreciation of them in person and writing to a degree that likely seems a bit overboard to them. Out of concern my past might come back again to haunt me once this book was published, I've shared my past experiences with just one co-worker who is a counselor. With her training, I knew she'd keep confidential anything I told her. I also knew she's heard it all before, and my story would not sound outlandish to her.

For me, it was a little awkward the first few times we encountered each other at work after I told her my story. But she treats me no different now than she did before. To have someone at work know my past and not use it against me or treat me differently has been such a relief. I no longer felt I was hiding something that would change everything for the worse if my colleagues found out. I didn't need to tell everyone. I just needed to hear from one person that if my past was known here, it wouldn't mess up the good thing I'd found.

Other differences in my current workplace are being greeted with a smile, being addressed by name, encountering humor in an environment that isn't often humorous. In return, I not only do my best to demonstrate appreciation for these daily spirit lifters, but I take pleasure in passing them on to others as well. Best of all is offering such encouragement to anyone who greets me with a scowl. They need it most.

Along with these external differences, an internal change has been necessary as well. Defining who I am by what I do for a living and how well I do it is now a thing of the past. Whether this change can be considered small is debatable. Changing our perspective on something isn't all that monumental. But our culture has intertwined self-worth with career success to the point where most people, especially men, see them as interdependent. Career success has become the measurement by which self-worth is gauged.

I remember feeling ashamed to tell people in my GROW support group that I had attempted suicide over career failure. But in reality, it was never about career failure. My issue wasn't losing a job, but losing my identity. After I shared my story in a Celebrate Recovery meeting, a man came up to thank me for explaining why job loss is such a big deal for men. The people in his life didn't understand that his own job loss went deeper than the job itself.

Our career will always be a part of what defines us. The problem is allowing it to define us so much that, should we lose our career, we don't know who we are. You may have seen the widely-aired Chevrolet commercial where one man asks another, "So what do you do?" What follows is a montage of the second man doing everything important to him, including family, friends, and fun, except what he actually does for a living. The point, of course, is that he isn't defined just by his job.

Isn't it sad that we so often answer this *what do you do* inquiry with a *where do I work* answer? Who is Steven Lomelino still includes what I do for a living. But how much that defines me has been overtaken by many other roles God has given me: spouse, father, son, uncle, brother, friend, worshipper, writer, football fan. And to think there was a time when I put employee at the top of this list!

What am I worth? One definition of worth is what someone is willing to pay to obtain something. Jesus gave his life for me. According to this definition, I am priceless just for whom I am. You are too.

At home, the numbers in my checkbook no longer control my emotions. All it takes to brighten my mood is for my son Shaun to notice I'm frustrated with something, usually the bills, and give me a hug. I may still feel a bit frustrated, but the frustration is now in proper perspective.

There are also still many things I'd like to have, but can't afford, especially the freedom to travel and enjoy activities away from home. Being unable to afford this can make me feel as though I'm under house arrest. But all I really need to satisfy me is a second-hand book from a thrift store or to pick up a cheap pack of football cards.

The truly important things in my life are no longer material possessions. They are moments spent experiencing life, good and bad, with family, friends, and anyone else God brings across my path. Walking down to the pond to fish is a mini-vacation. A walk around the neighborhood with Brenda is a special occasion.

The time I spend with God is indispensable. It's not like before when I turned to Christian radio for escape or strength to make it through another day or cried out to God for an immediate answer to my predicament. It is now a relationship that is more important than any human relationship. It is honest communication of my love of God for who He is. It is surrender of my plans for God's perfect plan. It is an outpouring of thanks for the new outlook on life God has given me. It is humility as I take on tasks He gives to me that I know I can do only with His strength and help.

Without God, life is meaningless. With Him, life is filled with endless possibilities regardless of my circumstances. With Him, each day is fresh and new. I am no longer running around in circles chasing after more and constantly discontent with the plenty I already have.

Do I still have big dreams? Yes, bigger than before. They are no longer focused on something I can attain, but how God can use me. I have no idea where God is taking my life, and it doesn't matter. Jesus tells us to seek first the kingdom of God and His righteousness, and all other things we need will be given to us as well (Matthew 6:33). God knows my every need and desire better than I know them myself. He has promised to meet my needs and that He will never leave me. Walking day by day with Him, I will accomplish something big, even if no one knows what that is but God Himself.

Spiritual Application

Don't hold back the small things you can give to God because you think they are too small to make any difference. Remember that God can use the little you offer to accomplish the humanly impossible. Little is much when placed in His hands.

Practical Application

You don't have to do something big to have a big impact on those around you. Small acts of kindness done on a regular basis may have more positive impact than bigger tasks done less frequently.

CHAPTER NINETEEN
SUCCESS REDEFINED

It is unfortunate that so many of us have to experience repeated failure before we are in the slightest bit inclined to let God define success for us. It took me seven years of failure to properly define success. It didn't need to take that long, since the best definition of success and how to achieve it isn't found in a dictionary, the Wall Street Journal, or some other business magazine. It is found in the owner's manual of life—the Holy Bible. In this chapter, we'll take a look at what scriptures written thousands of years ago have to say about 21st-century success.

So what does make someone a success? Nothing does. The proper question here is **Who** makes someone a success. Only God does. Then there is our part in attaining a successful life as defined by God, which requires following God's plan. As I referenced in the last chapter, Jesus Himself instructed:

Seek the Kingdom of God above all else, and live righteously, and he will give you everything you need (Matthew 6:33, NLT).

So God requires only two things of us—seek His kingdom and live righteously—in return for giving us everything we need? Yes, but those two things are lifetime commitments. They require self-sacrifice and living counter to our normal sinful human nature. There is also a lot involved in learning to put God first and treat other people right.

Also, it is God, not us, who decides what we need. That doesn't sound quite so appealing to our self-centered human mind. We need to recognize that only God can satisfy the desires of our hearts, both here on earth and for all eternity. Anything else is just jumping from one temporary, unfulfilling earthly "success" to another. Here are a few key steps necessary to seeking the Kingdom of God above all and living righteously:

Become a Child of God

But to all who believed him and accepted him, he gave the right to **become children of God** (John 1:12, NLT).

For you are all **children of God through faith in Christ Jesus** (Galatians 3:26, NLT).

If you try to hang on to your life, you will lose it. But if you give up your life for my sake and for the sake of the Good News, you will save it. And what do you benefit if you gain the whole world but lose **your own soul**? Is anything worth more than **your soul** (Mark 8:35-37, NLT)?

No amount of success can purchase eternal life for our soul. We all owe a sin debt that we cannot pay on our own. Without accepting the free gift of salvation through God's

Son, Jesus Christ, this life is nothing more than a game of Monopoly. And when the game is over, everything we've attained just goes back in the box, all of it. All that is left is our soul, and its fate lies in answering one question from the Ruler of the universe: "Who's paying your debt, My Son or you?"

Depend on God

David **continued to succeed in everything** he did, **for the LORD was with him** (1 Samuel 18:14, NLT).

Yes, I (God) am the vine; you are the branches. **Those who remain in Me**, and I in them, **will produce much** fruit. For apart from me you can do nothing (John 15:5).

All Christians claim to depend on God. But many, myself included, falter when God allows the things we actually depend on, such as full bank accounts and empty credit cards, to fail us. Where even more falter is when life is going so well that they develop an *I can take it from here* attitude. We need to depend on God through the good and the bad.

Seek the Kingdom of God

And if God cares so wonderfully for wildflowers that are here today and thrown into the fire tomorrow, he will certainly care for you. Why do you have so little faith? So don't worry about these things, saying, "What will we eat? What will we drink? What will we wear?" These things dominate the thoughts of unbelievers, but your heavenly Father already knows all your needs. **Seek the Kingdom of God above all else, and live righteously, and he will give you everything you need**. So don't worry about tomorrow, for tomorrow will bring its own worries. Today's trouble is enough for today (Matthew 6:30-34, NLT).

Throughout the gospels, we read that every facet of Jesus' life was to do the will of His Father. Though we can't come anywhere near the perfect way Jesus lived His life for the Kingdom of God, we can **seek** the Kingdom of God. Unfortunately, seeking to establish our own little kingdom tends to make seeking what God wants us to do to further His Kingdom an afterthought.

Accept God's Will for Your Life with an Attitude of Trust

Beware lest you say in your heart, "My power and the might of my hand have gotten me this wealth." You shall **remember the LORD your God, for it is He who gives you power to get wealth**. (Deuteronomy 8:16-17a, ESV).

Originally the title for this particular point ended with the word **contentment** instead of **trust**. I'm not minimizing the importance of contentment. But that requires less involvement and action than trust. I picture a father in a swimming pool with water up to his chest. His little girl stands shivering with fear on the safe, solid, familiar surface surrounding the pool, which is far too deep for her to manage. Meanwhile, her father is joyfully cheering and encouraging her to jump into the water.

The little girl can say truthfully how much she loves her father and appreciates all his love and care for her. But if she chooses contentment with familiar surroundings, to the edge of which her father has now brought her, over her father's desire for her to leave those familiar surroundings for a new, more exciting environment, she is sending her father a silent, but sure message: "I don't trust you if it means jumping into an unfamiliar, frightening, life-threatening environment."

What if the girl's father instead held her in his arms and walked from the shallow end into deeper water that is over her head? Again, she is exhibiting contentment, but no active trust. Her surroundings may be changing, but she is already safely in her father's arms as the water's depth gradually changes. Her experience tells her that her father has never dropped her and caused her harm up on solid ground, so she is confident he won't drop her and cause her harm in the water either. She has no new trust factor to overcome. She doesn't have to question what might happen if she jumps and goes under. Or if her father misses and she slips through his arms.

Before we beat up too much on this silly little girl, let's remember that we do the same thing. God has never promised us that if we take a leap in obedience, we won't go under. In fact, there are times when He lets us hit bottom. And in real life, that is much further than five feet down.

What God does promise us is that everything He allows us to experience is for our good and His glory, even if He doesn't protect us from failure, pain, or even death. A life of trust in God is a *no matter what happens* trust. There was a time when I prayed, "God, do whatever it takes to keep me close to You." Then God went places I wasn't willing to go. Places where I didn't trust Him with the results this could bring.

In the end, God did answer my prayer. Not by forcing me to jump, because God never forces us to trust Him. But by pulling all I was trusting in out from under my feet and allowing me to fall hard, fast, and far. After my fall, I was once again faced with the same question. Would I trust God? Or as in the scripture passage above, would I say in my heart,

"I define what success is, and with **the might of my hand** I will again attain it"?

Sadly, my answer was an ugly mix of both. My mouth said that I trusted God. But my heart said that I trusted God *plus* my own power. It was only through God's long-suffering grace that He finally brought me to the place where I could sincerely declare, "I trust God alone."

Emulate Jesus

Jesus saw the huge crowd as He stepped from the boat, **and He had compassion on them** and healed their sick (Matthew 14:14, NLT).

So now I (Jesus) am giving you a new commandment: **Love each other**. Just **as I have loved you**, you should love each other. Your love for one another will prove to the world that you are my disciples (John 13:34, 35).

Don't be selfish; don't try to impress others. **Be humble, thinking of others as better than yourselves**. Don't look out only for your own interests, but take an interest in others, too (Philippians 2:3, 4, NLT).

The famed 19th century English social thinker, philanthropist, and art critic John Ruskin once stated: "A man wrapped up in himself makes a very small parcel." Of all humanity, the only man who fully qualified or had any right to be wrapped up in Himself was Jesus Christ. Yet, throughout His entire ministry, Jesus wrapped Himself up in the lives of others.

In contrast, we get so caught up in our own lives that we leave no time available to invest in the lives of others. People won't know we are disciples of Jesus because we go to church regularly, tithe, pray, or read our Bible on the front porch for all to see. They will know we are His disciples because we love each other.

Do Not Worry, but Trust God, Delight in God, Be Still before God

Don't worry about the wicked or envy those who do wrong. For like grass, they soon fade away. Like spring flowers, they soon wither. Trust in the LORD and do good. Then you will live safely in the land and prosper. Take delight in the LORD, and he will give you your heart's desires. Commit everything you do to the LORD. Trust him, and he will help you. He will make your innocence radiate like the dawn, and the justice of your cause will shine like the noonday sun. Be still in the presence of the LORD, and wait patiently for him to act. Don't worry about evil people who prosper or fret about their wicked schemes. Stop being angry! Turn from your rage! Do not lose your temper—it only leads to harm. For the wicked will be destroyed, but those who trust in the LORD will possess the land . . . It is better to be godly and have little than to be evil and rich. For the strength of the wicked will be shattered, but the LORD takes care of the godly (Psalm 37:1-17, NLT)).

The above verses are only a portion of Psalm 37, which in its entirety, has had an immeasurable impact on my life. May I recommend that you take the time to read the entire psalm, either in the New Living Translation, as the portion given above, or another translation of your choice. Better yet, read it through in several different translations.

Second only to communicating my desperate state to others, following the instructions in this psalm would have gone a long way in preventing me from reaching the point of despair that makes suicide look like a viable option. My eyes and mind were fixed fully on what this psalm says not to do or worry about. Envy. The prosperity of others. Frustration with God's inaction. Anger. Rage. Having little. The strength of others. Feeling abandoned. Hard times. To sum it all up in one word: **injustice**.

In consequence, my eyes and mind were not fixed on what this psalm says I should have them fixed on. God's trustworthiness. God's loving watch-care over His children. His knowledge of the justice of my cause. Peace in God's presence. Prosperity as His child. His blessing. His guidance. To sum it all up in one word: **hope**.

Life may feel completely out of control, but you can trust that God has it completely in His control. If you are experiencing a bleak outlook on your life, take a deep breath, relax as best you can, and allow these healing, hopeful words to flow over you.

Spiritual Application

God defines what a successful life looks like. A story has been told of a man God asked to push a huge boulder. Each day this man faithfully went out and pushed the boulder. But at the end of each day, the boulder was exactly where it had been at the beginning.

When the man died and arrived in heaven, God told him, "Well done, good and faithful servant."

Surprised, the man asked God, "How can you tell me 'well done' when I never moved the boulder from its starting place?"

God replied, "I never asked you to move the boulder. I only asked you to push it, and that you did faithfully."

Practical Application

Put some serious thought into how you define success. Is that success worth the price, including the intangibles? If not, make changes to make your life truly successful.

CHAPTER TWENTY
THE POWER OF ONE

While I have lived out the events in this book, the story it tells is ultimately not about me. It is about the One who has the power to give life, appoint death, and Who is in control of every moment and experience in between.

Jesus Christ is the only reason this story is worth telling. He saved me from physical death on a roadside arc of gravel. He saved me from eternal death on the cross of Calvary. I pray that my own recovery may give you renewed hope. But it is only His death, burial, and resurrection that will give you eternal hope.

Without faith in Jesus, finding hope after my suicide attempt would have done no more than delay my physical death. I would still be chasing the insanity of success as defined by man. Most people will never attain the level of success they desire in this life. Many that do are still not satisfied. From the outside they seem to have it all, but without Jesus they have nothing that lasts beyond this life. How sad to think you have it all, then lose it all when you take your last breath. How glorious it is to give it all to Jesus and receive the rewards of a life lived for Him in eternity.

It may sound strange, but the only way to conquer life is to give up. Give up all control to the One who conquered death. Give up dependence on your own physical and mental capabilities. Life is complex, and death is inevitable. Mortal man can conquer neither without Jesus.

I enjoyed career success and what it could afford my family and me. I was content to stay at the job level I had reached. But God had far greater plans for me than to live a comfortable upper-middle class life. He wanted to give me the true desire of my heart, which was to live a life of purpose and meaning.

To get me there, God had to make me uncomfortable and discontent with the success I had attained. God saw where my life as I had planned it was going. He took the map I'd created and shredded it. I can thank Him for that now, but at the time I was devastated. I had made something of my life and could see good things ahead. With the power of one executive decision, out of my control, but perfectly in God's control, that life was gone.

That experience reminds me of a dream I once had. At the time, I was certain the dream was real. I had come into an obscenely-large amount of money. In my left hand, I held a tall, banded stack of hundred dollar bills. When I awoke, my left hand was still curled in the position of holding a large stack of paper money. But there was nothing in my hand. I looked at my empty hand and exclaimed out loud, "It was just there! I had it right there!"

Similarly, I had my life right there, only it was not a dream. There had been something in my grasp, and now I was empty-handed. My map was gone, and I was no longer sure where I was. Or even **who** I was anymore.

I am so glad God didn't let me live the life I planned. He has replaced it with one I could never have imagined. I have far less material wealth than I would have had if I had not lost the job at CIPS. I have a far better life though. By taking me through loss, depression, and mental anguish, God has equipped me to show others the way through their devastating times. Engaging in the lives of others gives me more satisfaction than any career success ever could. God has brought people into my life that have less than I did when I claimed to have lost everything. I want to help provide for their needs, and God may eventually put me in a position to do so. For now, God wants us to depend on Him. With the power of the One, Jesus Christ, I need not fear anything this life brings my way.

Spiritual Application

One man, Jesus Christ, lived on this earth for thirty-three years and made a way for all mankind to live eternally in heaven. His life, death, burial, and resurrection brought eternal hope by conquering sin and death once for all. Holding on to this hope provides all the hope we need to live a joyful, abundant life in all circumstances.

Practical Application

One person, you, has the potential to make a great difference in the world around you. The unpopular choice to live your life in a way that elevates others instead of yourself makes life better for everyone your life touches. You may not see any big dividends from investing in others, but the multitude of small positive influences on others you have over the course of your life has a much greater impact than you will ever realize.

CHAPTER TWENTY-ONE

180 DEGREES

I know what it's like to be alive. Truly, abundantly, fully alive. In fact, God has turned me 180 degrees. Only He could do a work so miraculous in me that I can now see a 180-degree turn **away from** my dreams as the only way to attain the desires of my heart. I hold tight the words of Psalms 37: 4, 5:

Delight thyself also in the LORD: and He shall give thee the desires of thine heart. Commit thy way unto the LORD; trust also in Him; and He shall bring it to pass (KJV).

Without these verses and the rest of God's Word, I would be turned back around in a moment. God has taken me from not understanding at all what these verses mean to misunderstanding to a clear understanding now of their meaning. Let's take a closer look at some of the individual words of this passage.

Delight

How do you delight in the Lord? I delight in plenty of other things. So why is delight in the Lord such a hard concept? The tendency to over-spiritualize anything having to do with God made me think I needed some righteous prayer or act to show God my delight in Him. But God has taught me that what this means is to simply delight in Him more than I delight in anyone or anything else. That said, simply delighting in God most of all is not that simple.

Commit

Who commits to anything? That implies forever. No turning back. No thirty-day trial. Like a cliff dive, you either do it or you don't. You don't dive, then change your mind in mid-air. You're either all in or all out. There is no pre-nuptial. There is no escape clause.

In fact, there is nothing worse than having one foot on the water and one foot in the boat. When Jesus called Peter to walk on water in the Sea of Galilee, Peter could have frozen half-way out of the boat. But he took the leap of faith to walk towards Jesus on the water (Matthew 14: 22-33). Likewise, Jesus wants you to either admit completely you're too afraid to step out on the water with Him or trust completely that all you have to do to walk on water is keep your eyes fixed on Him.

I have done what is impossible for a simple man like me. That is when I am most alive. I have also done what is natural for a simple man like me and focused my attention on the waves. That is when I am least alive. Either way, I have walked away from the boat. There is no such thing as being out of the boat, but still close enough to jump back in if you panic. Water gives you nothing to push off of, so you may as well turn your back to the boat, face Jesus, and start walking until He says you've arrived with the words every Christian should long to hear: "Well done."

Trust

Is anyone worthy of trust? Not on this earth. Especially when we are asked to walk by faith, not by sight. Human wisdom says we need to hold on to something tangible. God says let go of it. Are you at the end of your rope? It's more painful to hold on than it is to let go. But letting go requires trust in someone who can handle the consequences of you no longer having whatever you let go of. Only the Holy Trinity—God the Father, Son, and Holy Spirit—is worthy of that kind of trust.

Desires

Humanly speaking, our desires cannot be forever fulfilled. The void you try to fill with the "desires of thine heart" is a bottomless pit. All attempts to fill it lead to frustration and hopelessness. What are the desires of every human heart? We all want to live a life of purpose. We want to leave a legacy. We want to love and to be loved. The only way to attain those desires is to align our plans and goals for our lives with God's.

And that requires a 180-degree turn, no less, no greater. In other words, the shortest route to God's abundant life is a straight line in the exact opposite direction than our human nature takes us. God continues to call us to make that turn even as we drift off the narrow path, meander down dead ends, walk in circles, or just plain stop. Why God cares so deeply that He won't give up on us is beyond my comprehension. Thank God for His patience with us.

He Shall

It does not depend on me. What a relief! The theme of most recovery books is never give up. This one says do a 180. Give up. Give up living life in your own strength. You will fail. Want to find your life? Lose it. Want to fulfill your purpose in life? Fulfill God's purpose for your life. Want to leave a legacy? Live to pass down the example of a life lived for what is of eternal value instead of living to obtain and pass down temporary things. Want to love and be loved? Love the Lord your God with all you are and love your neighbor as yourself, and He shall bring it to pass.

When I started this chapter, I foolishly thought I could put everything God thinks that is 180 degrees opposite what man thinks in one chapter. Then I thought, again foolishly, that I could do it in an entire book. I've come to recognize I could not accomplish that feat if I kept writing without pause for a hundred lifetimes. God thinks 180 degrees the opposite of our human nature, period, paragraph, the end.

But here are just a few examples that come to mind. Let's call these the tip of the largest iceberg our minds can picture. Then let's admit we're still nowhere close.

> What we think of as wealth, God knows is poverty.
> What we think of as righteous deeds, God knows are filthy rags.
> What we think of as loss, God knows is gain.

What we think of as freedom, God knows is
   slavery.
What we think of as power, God knows is
   weakness.
What we think of as intelligence, God knows is
   ignorance.
What we think of as life, God knows leads to
   death.
What we think of as ours, God knows is His.
We want instant gratification. God says wait.
We are selfish. God desires selflessness.
We want to keep. God wants us to share.
We want to hate. God wants us to love.
We want to get even. God wants us to return
   good for evil.
We seek to be first. Jesus says to be first we
   must be last and servant of all.

This gives me a new perspective on the fact that His ways are not our ways and His thoughts are higher than our thoughts (Isaiah 55:8-9).

I have retained one from my short list of ways that God's thoughts are higher than our thoughts for special consideration. It is what I told my youngest son when he accepted Christ as Lord and Savior. And that is this. The more you let go, the more you had better hold on for the ride of your life—literally. God's plan is an exciting, fulfilling life that will take you places beyond your imagination.

Spiritual Application

God does have a plan for your life, and that plan is a better, more fulfilling plan than you could ever dream up. Writing this book was the furthest thing from my mind when thinking about what I wanted to do with my life. It has been a spectacular experience watching God connect the dots. Let me list those dots chronologically.

A California writer gets *Insane Success* rolling by taking me under her wing with encouragement, advice, and editing at no cost, simply because she felt compelled by God to do so. One bit of advice was to attend a Christian writer's conference. Thank you, Sue Tornai.

Kentucky writers keep *Insane Success* rolling with more encouragement, advice, and much needed connections. Thanks you, staff and attendees of the 2014 Kentucky Christian Writer's Conference.

An Illinois writer keeps *Insane Success* rolling after turning down my request to edit it by leading me to the Christian Editor Connection website. Thanks so much, Jeanette Levellie.

The CEC keeps *Insane Success* rolling by having six of its members show interest. I was hoping to get one, and God blessed me with six. What a day of celebration that was for me. Then came the difficult part. Which of the six did God have planned for me to work with? And how do I choose? Let's see, there are six sides on a die . . . no, no, no! Prayer, research, more prayer, listening for God's still small voice, even more prayer, contact with the editors, and still more prayer was needed. Why couldn't there be someone close to make the decision easy? Distance, that's it! Which editor has experience working at a distance from the writer? That answer was easy, the one who had worked from the United States with a writer in Chile. If she can work across continents, she can work across states. Thanks, Kathy Ide, for founding the Christian Editor Connection.

My first choice, an author and editor currently living in Pennsylvania, keeps *Insane Success* rolling by saying yes to a manuscript that was only half there and giving this green, in-over-his-head, don't-wanna-be (but God did want me to be) writer the opportunity to complete it under her long-distance tutelage. I have only been more excited about one other "yes" in my life, and that was to my marriage proposal. Thanks, Jeanette Windle.

Between each dot, I thought *dead end.* At times I even hoped for that, because I was so out of my comfort zone. Then God would miraculously connect one impossible dot to the next impossible dot. If you think I'm overstating God's role in all this, who but God connects Illinois to California to Kentucky to Illinois to California to Pennsylvania and makes every step move the project forward? When God gives you a task to do, He will make it happen through you.

Practical Application

If your life is going in the complete opposite direction from what you have planned for it, don't try to force it to reverse course. It may eventually come back to where you want it to go. But you will need to give it some time. And if it doesn't come back around to where you want it, you will likely find yourself glad that it didn't.

CHAPTER TWENTY-TWO
THE PERFECT ENDING

It is now 2017, a full decade since I found hope at Hope Institute. Almost all the pieces of my life have fallen back into place except . . .

There is a song by the Christian music group Tenth Avenue North from their album *The Struggle* that still nearly brings me to tears. The song is called "Worn", and one line in particular is repeated in each stanza: "Let me see redemption win, let me know the struggle ends."

Yes, the struggle continues, and we cannot at this point see any end in sight. Or as the song puts it, "Life just won't let up!"

The biggest struggle continues to be keeping our head above water financially. Sometimes I connect the dots all the way back to the CIPS/UE merger and try to calculate my total dollars-and-cents loss of that one event, if my income had continued to rise from nearly $17 an hour in the early 90s instead of still being today nearly two dollars per hour shy of what I was making over two decades ago. Other times I think, *We've gone from how can one family have so many unjust employment losses one after another to how can one family have so many major medical issues one after another!*

I don't want to overstate our medical woes because I know how healthy we are overall. But just take pancreatitis that nearly kills you after thinking it was a kidney stone and add your wife getting a checkup because she wants to see a foot specialist, only to discover she needs her gall bladder removed. Then that kidney stone shows up after all and has to be surgically removed. After the gall bladder, your wife gets around to seeing that foot specialist, once again needs surgery, and misses eight weeks of work, three of them unpaid. Then you require hernia surgery before she can return to work. By that point, you begin to wonder, *What's going on? I think we've met our lifetime quota for injustice and misfortune, God!*

And that was how 2015 ended for our family. Then out of nowhere, someone I hadn't heard from since the mid-2000's sent me a message about a job opportunity in downtown Springfield that involved essentially getting paid for doing the same thing I was doing as a volunteer for GROW. The big difference was that I would help emotionally hurting people over the phone instead of in person.

I was told that the position paid $10,000 a year more than I was currently making. My instinctive thought was that this was finally the God-orchestrated perfect ending I'd been waiting for that would make sense out of everything that had happened before, including the complete mismatch of a Call Center job and a year dealing with workplace harassment.

I found myself torn. I loved everything about my current job except the pay. But this new opportunity seemed like a perfect fit. In fact, all those employment-hell years now seemed like the perfect training for this job opportunity. And it would certainly help us financially.

To my thinking, the decision was only a matter of my picking one job over the other, since I had three distinct advantages over the other applicants. First, someone already working in the position had recommended me to the supervisor doing the hiring. Second, they were replacing a male, and most of the applicants were female. Third, the supervisor was taking input from the three people already working the position, and I already had a guaranteed vote from one of them.

I was so confident I'd get a job offer that I spoke to my boss, letting her know I was torn, but that I was checking further into the job opportunity and would definitely be applying for it if I didn't find anything negative to sway my decision. From there, everything went great. A forty-five-minute phone interview led to an evening of pre-placement testing. That led to a two-hour in-person interview. The final piece of my puzzle was about to fall into place. Redemption would win. The struggle would end.

But then came—nothing! No call back. No job offer. After a couple weeks of anxious waiting, I couldn't take it anymore and placed a follow-up call. I was not expecting the cheerful voice that responded, "I'm so glad you called. I've been meaning to get back to you to let you know another applicant was chosen."

I can state honestly that I have never been so shocked, and I've had plenty of opportunities to be shocked. I have also never been so happy that I'd applied the lesson of not setting up a win-lose situation. Instead, I'd gone in with a win-win attitude, acknowledging that it was God's decision to open or close that door and thanking Him in advance for whatever decision He chose. It was still a shock, but not the devastating blow I could have set myself up for.

Spiritual Application

What looks God-orchestrated isn't always God-orchestrated. If I had convinced myself 100% that this was God's hand putting the final piece into place, I would have had a major problem to deal with when I wasn't selected. The question that rose to my mind, but I immediately and easily dismissed, would have presented a major conundrum. Had God just dangled the perfect ending in front of my face, then yanked it away as though taunting, "Is this what you're looking for? Ha, ha, you can't have it!"?

No, He did not. God knew what was best for me and never gave me the opportunity to make a bad decision.

Practical Application

Some Christian media may try to convince you otherwise, but genuine faith in Jesus Christ and obedience to God does not mean all the pieces fall neatly back into place this side of heaven. Do not set your expectations so high that everything short of them is failure.

Chapter Twenty-Three
Abundant Life after Loss

I finished ten years at Hope Institute in November, 2016. While it has been nice to reach double digits of years with the same employer again, I know now that longevity does not equal security. Brenda and I, as well as our younger son who is still living at home, remain active members of the same church. Five years ago, after forty-eight years under the same pastor, our church brought in a new senior pastor. Under both pastors, my spiritual growth has been a steady pace of growing closer to God by regularly spending time with Him through Scripture, prayer, worship, and fellowship with my brothers and sisters in Christ.

Financially, I tithed fairly regularly during 2014, but reneged when money was tight. At the start of 2015, I made a vow to God that if things got tight financially, something else would have to give instead of His rightful tithe. When things got tight, I held true to my vow. I cut back on cable TV. I had my youngest son start paying for his health insurance. I also made some changes to my own health insurance. Typically, by the latter months of any given year, I have "borrowed" from the tithe so much that there is no possibility of catching up. But by the end of 2015, I am thrilled to say that Brenda and I had tithed both of our gross incomes for an entire year for the first time ever.

I don't mention my failure to tithe to garner sympathy regarding our financial state. Nor do I mention my success in tithing to garner accolades. I mention both mainly to point out that every Christian should tithe simply in obedience to God. This is the means God has put in place to spread the Gospel. And however valid, humanly speaking, the reasons we may give for not tithing, God has provided no exceptions to this command.

It basically boils down to deciding if God comes first in my finances or I do. Though I would love for this book to provide an influx of money to get us around that ever-elusive corner, the purpose in writing this book has never been financial gain. Every author I've asked about the odds of breaking even or making money on a book has told me there is simply no way to know how a book will fare. Whether or not God blesses me financially because of my obedience in writing this, He had a reason for me to write it.

I may never fully know what that reason is. But again, it boils down to simple obedience without regard for what's in it for me. Finances are most definitely the single greatest hurdle for me to get—and stay—over. Most likely because of the constant reminders from my empty wallet, low checkbook balance, and barely fair credit score. Still, I would not trade the spiritual growth and God's maturing of me in areas that have made me mentally stronger, more compassionate, and a less self-centered man. Some areas where I've seen spiritual growth include:

Pride

Pride detox is brutal when it gets as bad as I let it get. I will never fully free myself of pride this side of heaven. I will, however, never again allow pride to factor into my decision-making. My pride tells me to keep my depression and suicide attempt a secret. Christ's compassion for me compels me to have compassion for others. And that includes sharing with them that I couldn't pull myself out of the pit of despair either. God had to pull me out.

Daily Dependence

I have never been spiritually stronger than when I literally put my entire life in God's hands. God has taught me that this isn't a once-and-done event. I am now a living sacrifice (Romans 12:1-2), and each day I have to overcome the temptation to climb off the altar and start living for myself again.

Love

There is an old song by the 1970s British-American rock band *Foreigner* titled, "I Want to Know What Love Is". Until I experienced God's love for me, I may have thought I knew what love was and that I knew how to love others. But I didn't. God has taught me that love isn't mainly a feeling or emotion. It is a conscious choice to love others, even when they choose to hate me. This means I have to forgive injustice, not avenge it.

I have also learned that love is a verb. My action or inaction lets people know if I love them or not. My nature is to love myself and those who love me. Unlike that *Foreigner* song, in order to truly love others as Christ requires, I don't need to know **what** love is as much as I need to know **Who** love is. God is the only source of genuine love. In fact, the Bible tells us that God *is* love (1 John 4:8). If I don't know God, I don't have His love to share with others.

Other examples of God maturing me as a man include:

Relationships

I still need time to myself, but I am not nearly as resentful of others cutting in on my personal time as I once was. Learning to allow someone else to bear my burden with me and experiencing the great relief that provides makes me want to bear others' burdens with them. This requires more than the shallow relationships I once had. The deeper my relationships are, the more I am willing to give of myself, even of my precious time.

Frustration

My life now has just as much frustration as before. The source of most of my frustration is no longer job loss. What is most frustrating now is the limitations job loss has created. September, 2015, was one incident that could have frustrated me to tears. Brenda and I wanted to take our son to a St. Louis Cardinals baseball game for his birthday. I could get decent seats for under $20, and Busch Stadium is close enough to Springfield to go down and back the same day.

Unfortunately, our financial situation didn't allow this to happen. In prior years, I would have done it anyway and made our already frustrating financial situation worse. I can't say I was not at all frustrated by this. But I have learned to make the best of what God has given me to work with. I used to say that I hated special occasions because they reminded me of how much I didn't have or couldn't do. But not being able to do what I want no longer dampens the occasion for me as it once did.

That same month, we had back-to-back-to-back problems with our car transmission, a leak/mold discovery in our home, and an ant invasion. Trying to stay on a positive subject, I asked Brenda if it was too early to start planning a thirtieth wedding anniversary getaway. Upon which she reminded me that our thirtieth was less than six months away, not eighteen as I was thinking. Meaning a grand getaway wasn't going to happen.

I was more than a little dismayed since our last grand getaway, a week in the Long Beach California area, had been ten years prior and was also our first grand getaway as a couple. Our twenty-years-late honeymoon, you could call it. But again, the lack of a grand getaway doesn't make thirty years of marriage any less of a milestone.

Finances

It is a bit ironic that finances, one of the major contributors that brought me to the point of despair in 2004, hasn't improved much. That whole make-progress, start-over cycle, though now caused by something other than job loss, is still occurring. If I were still basing my value and level of success using human definitions, I would still consider myself of very little value and hopeless as far being successful.

But the hope I have is not because God led me to a steady job. In fact, there is no guarantee that I won't lose my current job. I don't know for sure how I would respond if that should happen, but I trust that my confidence in God has reached a point that I would not lose faith in Him as I did before. I have hope because God has brought me from seeing death as my only solution to seeing that God is completely in control even if I am presented with a situation for which I have no solution, and He already knows the way through my situation.

If you are currently in what you see as a hopeless situation, God has already begun leading you through it by placing this book in your hands. This book is not the solution. It simply tells you that there is a solution. That there is hope available for you. If you are having or have had suicidal thoughts, let God lead you to the same hope to which He lead me. Before those thoughts become action, reach out to at least one of the many people God has put on this earth to walk beside you toward abundant life after loss.

Spiritual Application

At the end of 2014, boxes of tithe envelopes were set out as usual at our church for members to pick up. At that point, Brenda and I were in no better shape financially than we had been when I'd decided we couldn't tithe again until we climbed out of the hole that decisions within our control and losses outside our control had put us in. Seeing the envelopes brought to mind the inconsistency of my giving and spiritual life in general.

At the heart of all this was the matter of control. It seemed that even decisions within our control were based so much on the unknown that we had no control over whether the outcome would be positive, and even good decisions were at times leading to bad results. Those losses outside our control drove home even more so just how little control we actually have over the path our lives will take.

I don't have control over my own life, I thought to myself, *and yet I'm trying to keep our financial situation under control by cutting my support of God's church. I know God is in control of everything, including my life, and He never has to make decisions based on the unknown. So how is it I still think I can do a better job than God?*

If I started tithing again, I knew I could no longer use this money as a control valve that I could dial back any time the pressure of not having enough money to cover expenses became too great. I would have to decide here and now whether I was willing to dial back somewhere else. Knowing that making this type of promise to God in no way obligated Him to make my life go well made the decision all the harder. But I also knew just how much God had brought me through, so I surrendered to His control with the added pledge to never again push Him off the throne of my life.

At a Bible study in June, 2015, my pastor asked for prayer requests. I related this decision to the group and asked for prayer regarding our finances. The pastor asked me if I was staying true to my promise to God. I gave him a big smile, so happy to be able to say yes. But even happier that through his question, my pastor was assuring me that God had it all under control.

Practical Application

At the center of many, if not all, of our conflicts, is the question of who is in control. I came to the point where it seemed taking my life was the only way to regain control of it, because at that moment every aspect of my life seemed under the control of someone or something else. If you feel this way, you need to remember that the only person anyone can control is themself. The only way others can control you is by your consent, unless you are being controlled by violent force or threat of violent force, which is a crime.

If you are controlled by circumstances and feel you are in a lose-lose situation, ask yourself what your elusive third option is. Or better yet, ask someone to join you in answering that question. The answer may seem so drastic at first that you don't even consider it an option. But weighed against remaining in a bad situation that is continually eating away at you, taking drastic measures to correct the situation may provide a way back to living your life versus allowing someone or something else to have control over it.

I should clarify that my use of the word **drastic** does not suggest taking back control by any means that creates an irreversible worse situation, such as suicide, murder, abortion, theft, or violence. Taking a life or committing a vengeful act is never the elusive third option. But taking a seemingly unrecoverable step backward probably won't end as horrifically as the panic-driven worst case scenario playing out in your mind. I believed without a doubt if I left Linq we would lose everything and be living on the streets. I won't deny that leaving did involve a lot of loss and struggle. But it was nothing close to the immediate collapse I had envisioned.

EPILOGUE
SAYING "YES" TO GOD'S DIVINE PLAN

2 Corinthians 1:3, 4 summarizes perfectly my primary purpose in writing this book:

All praise to God, the Father of our Lord Jesus Christ. God is our merciful Father and the source of all comfort. He comforts us in all our troubles so that we can comfort others. When they are troubled, we will be able to give them the same comfort God has given us (NLT).

On November 4, 2004, when I had given up on God, He had not given up on me. He showed me mercy on what was supposed to be the day of my death. He then comforted me, at times through His Spirit, but mostly through bringing people alongside me whom He had comforted in their time of trouble.

I also said no a lot that day. If I could live that day over again, I would say still say no to my employer, but in a much different manner. That day would then change dramatically. Instead of running away by saying no to my wife and God, I would run to them.

That would not have changed the fact that I was still in desperate need of ending my turmoil. However, by running to God, I could have tapped into His unfailing source of hope and strength. Only then would I have been able to reach out of the darkness and find the hands of the people I'd shut out for far too long. This would have provided a much better starting point for my recovery process. I sincerely believe that if I'd killed my pride instead of trying to kill myself, my recovery would have been much shorter.

If there is one thing I have learned from my experiences, it is that God has a divine plan for my life. His plan goes beyond the seeming success of those who appear to have their every dream come true. It goes beyond the seeming success of those with ostensibly inexhaustible wealth. In truth, a lifetime spent seeking that type of success is a far greater insanity than that which prompted me to attempt to take my own life. In contrast, God's plan has taken me to a level of awe and wonder of Him that obliterates my once covetous and adulating view of those who are insanely successful by human standards.

Saying yes to God's plan for my life doesn't bring about heaven on earth. But it does bring meaning, hope, and joy that allows me to live above my circumstances. Choosing to say yes to God is the best decision I've ever made. It's not a once-and-done decision, though. Every day I have a choice to live according to my plans or live according to His. This side of heaven, I will never live perfectly according to His plans for me. But when I fail, which is often, He is there with forgiveness, mercy, and compassion to put me back on the right course.

Everyone experiences times of despair, failure, and doubt. God cares. It may feel like God hates you. But that is not true. God loves you. Your life may feel pointless. But God has a divine plan for your life. Make the best decision of your life. Say yes to God and begin to experience the abundant life God has planned for you. In so doing, you will discover, as I have, real success God's way. Amazing success. ***Insane success.***

APPENDIX
PRAYING THROUGH DIFFICULTIES

When we are praying in times of difficulty, there are three critical presuppositions we need to keep in mind:

God is Perfect

God's way is perfect. All the LORD's promises prove true. He is a shield for all who look to him for protection (Psalms 18:30, NLT).

He is the Rock; his deeds are perfect. Everything he does is just and fair. He is a faithful God who does no wrong; how just and upright he is (Deuteronomy 32:4, NLT).

God is Good

We know how much God loves us, and we have put our trust in his love. God is love, and all who live in love live in God, and God lives in them (1 John 4:16, NLT).

God is in control.

Dear brothers and sisters, when troubles of any kind come your way, consider it an opportunity for great joy. ³ For you know that when your faith is tested, your endurance has a chance to grow. ⁴ So let it grow, for when your endurance is fully developed, you will be perfect and complete, needing nothing (James 1:2-4, NLT).

While praying for God to remove the difficulty is not necessarily wrong, perhaps we should also or at times instead pray for:

Perseverance, Maturity, Growth

Dear brothers and sisters, when troubles of any kind come your way, consider it an opportunity for great joy. ³ For you know that when your faith is tested, your endurance has a chance to grow. ⁴ So let it grow, for when your endurance is fully developed, you will be perfect and complete, needing nothing (James 1:2-4, NLT).

Knowledge of God's will

So we have not stopped praying for you since we first heard about you. We ask God to give you complete knowledge of his will and to give you spiritual wisdom and understanding. ¹⁰ Then the way you live will always honor and please the Lord, and your lives will produce every kind of good fruit. All the while, you will grow as you learn to know God better and better (Colossians 1:9, NLT).

Godly Living/Holiness

Because we have these promises, dear friends, let us cleanse ourselves from everything that can defile our body or spirit. And let us work toward complete holiness because we fear God (2 Corinthians 13:7, NLT).

Consistent Christian Walk

Then the way you live will always honor and please the Lord, and your lives will produce every kind of good fruit. All the while, you will grow as you learn to know God better and better (Colossians 1:10, NLT).

Service to Christ

So we keep on praying for you, asking our God to enable you to live a life worthy of his call. May he give you the power to accomplish all the good things your faith prompts you to do (2 Thessalonians 1:11, NLT).

Greater Wisdom and Understanding

So we have not stopped praying for you since we first heard about you. We ask God to give you complete knowledge of his will and to give you spiritual wisdom and understanding (Colossians 1:9, NLT).

Witnessing Opportunities

And I am praying that you will put into action the generosity that comes from your faith as you understand and experience all the good things we have in Christ (Philemon 1:6, NLT).

Spiritual Strength

Now may our Lord Jesus Christ himself and God our Father, who loved us and by his grace gave us eternal comfort and a wonderful hope,[17] comfort you and strengthen you in every good thing you do and say (2 Thessalonians 2:16-17, NLT).

Discernment of God's Will

I pray that your love will overflow more and more, and that you will keep on growing in knowledge and understanding. For I want you to understand what really matters, so that you may live pure and blameless lives until the day of Christ's return (Philippians 1:9-10, NLT).

Deeper Knowledge of God

Asking God, the glorious Father of our Lord Jesus Christ, to give you spiritual wisdom and insight so that you might grow in your knowledge of God (Ephesians 1:17, NLT).

Recognition of our Riches in God

I pray that your hearts will be flooded with light so that you can understand the confident hope he has given to those he called—his holy people who are his rich and glorious inheritance (Ephesians 1:18, NLT).

Awareness of God's Power in Us

I pray that your hearts will be flooded with light so that you can understand the confident hope he has given to those he called—his holy people who are his rich and glorious inheritance (Ephesians 1:18, NLT).

More Love for Other Christians

And may the Lord make your love for one another and for all people grow and overflow, just as our love for you overflows (1 Thessalonians 3:12, NLT).

Unity in the Church

May God, who gives this patience and encouragement, help you live in complete harmony with each other, as is fitting for followers of Christ Jesus. Then all of you can join together with one voice, giving praise and glory to God, the Father of our Lord Jesus Christ (Romans 15:5-6, NLT).

*From "Praying Through Difficulties", Bible study handout, by Pastor David Fox, Grace Baptist Church, Springfield, IL used by permission.

ABOUT THE AUTHOR

Steven Lomelino is a Christian, family man, suicide prevention supporter, and NFL fan - Go Raiders! - who lives in Springfield, IL with his wife, Brenda. He also works at Hope (employer and attitude).

Made in the USA
Lexington, KY
18 May 2017